# Saint Theresa
# The Saint of Ecstasy

## René Fülöp-Miller

Donald Castellano-Hoyt, Publisher

dcastellano.hoyt@gmail.com

With St. Theresa there appears in the circle of saints a woman whose sainthood was imposed upon her by God. Her experience of God came to her in a state of ecstatic rapture and overwhelmed her with elemental force.

In the extraordinary life of this saint natural events crossed .over into supernatural spheres, worldly and heavenly orders met, visions emerged from perception, the sound of human voices was taken up by heavenly calls and the fragile human frame served in ecstatic moments as the vessel of God's abundance.

In Theresa we are confronted with a resident of two realms, at home in heaven and on earth, and constantly moving to and from the spatial confines of a little Spanish town and the infinite space of eternity. The clock of the convent struck the hours; but for Theresa it would suddenly grow silent; time would cease; timelessness would surround her. And often it was but a flash that separated her daily routine from motionless rest in God.

The contrast between the natural and the supernatural which is so strikingly manifest in Theresa's dual existence was further intensified by the time in which she was born. It was a time of progressive secularization.

The castles, cathedrals, convents and monasteries, the fortified cities and towns, which had protected the introspective quiet of medieval life against the onslaught of worldly interference, were still standing with their ramparts, their turrets and cloisters, but they seemed now to have survived merely as memorials of what they had actually been in the past.

Theresa's century was no longer part of the era of transition from the Middle Ages to modern times; it was in every respect the new beginning itself. Within a few decades—and these were precisely the decades of Theresa's life—the expansive energies of modern activism increased the size of the earth by continents. North America had just been discovered. Cortes had conquered Mexico and crossed the Isthmus of Panama. Magellan sailed around the southern tip of the new world and discovered the Philippines. The earth began to assume the shape of a globe, and the treasures which the conquistadors brought home from overseas increased the wealth of the old world.

Power was the ideal of conquering worldliness. It was the time in which the idea of world dominion, of modern imperialism, was born.

This trend of secularization cast its spell also over man's spiritual pursuits. No longer did he look within himself. He looked around himself, and what he saw there, absorbed his attention and spurred his mind to inquire and examine. The earth, the here and the now, had displaced the heavens beyond.

Undreamed-of continents of human knowledge were discovered. Treasures of learning were brought together for the use of future times.

The sixteenth century saw the world as the tangible reality of conquered domains, continents discovered, oceans traversed and treasures won for carefree enjoyment, but also as a world of science, as the opening up of the truth about things.

And this time, when the outer world achieved such glorious triumphs in all its spheres, was precisely the time when no less glorious triumphs were achieved through Theresa of Ávila by the world hat lies within: a world without space and yet more spacious; without gold and dominions and none the less richer; without con-p tests but yet in possession of greater safety; a world without time but of more lasting permanence; without tangible form but not therefore less real than the newly conquered terrestrial globe.

Magellan's Vittoria, the first ship to sail around the earth, had just returned, after an absence of several years, to its home port in Spain, when a nun, returning from a trip around the world of the soul, emerged in her cell from the timelessness of ecstatic rapture to join her companions in the parlor of her convent at Ávila.

The conquistadors had seen America, India, Java, Panama; she had seen infinity. Ships laden with gold returned from conquered new worlds to the golden gate at the mouth of the Guadalquivir; she returned to earth from visions of the kingdom of heaven, laden with bliss which the hull of no ship could carry.

To a world ruled by power she opposed her inner world, conquered in powerless rapture and ruled by self-deposition. Complete self-deposition was the foundation of her true kingdom of God.

To a world that indulged in distraction and chatter she brought news from a world in which utter concentration, unspoken, spiritual prayer imparted the highest bliss.

Her truth was an antithesis to the new truth of science. Sense perception was the scientist's road to truth; measuring reason served as his check; experiments offered proof. Vision outside the sphere of the senses was Theresa's road to certainty; immeasurable feeling was her check; mystic experience contributed proof.

A world of data and a world of vision confronted each other as rivals. Copernicus had explored the universe by means of his astronomical calculations. He had come to the conclusion that the sun is the center of our world. The earth had been demoted. It was a mere satellite and no longer the center of creation. Man was no longer the lord of creation but merely the ruler of the earth.

St. Theresa had explored the universe of the soul by means of her ecstatic visions, and she had come to the conclusion that the ultimate center around which the suns and the earths revolve, lies in the depths of the human soul. In rivalry with the Copernican discovery of the sun as the center of creation, Theresa discovered the astronomy of the soul and found God, the creator and sun of suns, in the soul of man. Man was the A and O of all that exists.

Theresa's contemporary Kepler discovered the laws of gravity for material bodies; she discovered them for the soul.

Vesalius, the young anatomist at Basle, opened a human corpse and studied the organs within. Theresa, the nun of Ávila, laid bare the one imperishable thing in man: his soul. Servet discovered the lesser circulation of the blood which nourishes the body. Theresa discovered the greater circulation of divine enlightenment which nourishes the soul.

The first precision clock had just been constructed. The course of time began to be measured in minutes, and for the first time church bells rang out each quarter of the hour. But Theresa experienced the indivisibility of time which cannot pass because its measure is eternity.

The century, entranced in a delirium of cold reason, was challenged by a Spanish nun who rose to superhuman greatness in the enchantment of timeless visions.

The universal power of the church had been severely shaken. In the year of Theresa's birth Luther proclaimed his schism. Calvin made of Geneva a second Rome. Henry VIII had founded his own church, and Mary Queen of Scots submitted humbly to the dictates of the heretic John Knox.

The old forms of dogmatic piety had lost much of their rigor under the onslaught of science and other forces of secularization. In defense of Catholicism kings took up arms and popular preachers tried to fortify the faith by threats of punishment and hellish torture in the realm beyond the grave. At the Council of Trent cardinals, bishops and theologians convened in order to settle the question of a new codification of the Catholic dogma. An organized army of trained soldiers of God was led by Ignatius of Loyola into the great decisive battle against the forces of the Reformation. The doctors of the church cited their sacred authorities or tried, by the more timely means of rational proofs of God, to strengthen the old faith.

St. Theresa wrote down what she had learned in the quiet solitude of her cell, beyond the confusion of time and space, beyond dogma and rational demonstration, beyond her own comprehension and the perception of her senses. She wrote of the visits of her invisible Lord and of His will which He communicated to her in inaudible words.

The declining church derived from it new energies, a new vitality that emanated from the deepest depths of the experience of faith, from the true source of all piety, from direct contact with God.

For the church of this time Christ had come to be merely an allegorical label, an object of the creed and a topic of theological disputes. Through Theresa the church learned once again about Christ as a living reality, about the Christ whom the disciples saw on the road to Emmaus, whom Saul of Tarsus had met on his way to Damascus, the Christ in whom the faith of the church had begun, in whose spirit it had been renewed by St. Francis of Assisi.

Ávila, where St. Theresa was born in March, 1515, was a little town of old Castile, one of those monuments of stone which had survived into modern times as a reminder of the past.

It lay in the hills of the Sierra de Guadarrama on the banks of the Adaja, and with its heavy walls it had been, throughout the Middle Ages, a mighty bulwark of Spanish Christendom against the threatening onslaught of the Moors. Its streets were narrow and winding. Its houses, built of dark stones, had been the homes of knights who slept with their swords at their sides, for they had to be ready, when the tocsin tolled, to ward off the raiding infidels, And in all parts of the town there were churches, monasteries and sacred monuments. There was scarcely a stone which had not been sanctified by martyrdom or miracle. Ávila was a town of stones and saints. *Ávila cantos y santos*, as the saying went.

For a hundred years now the tocsin in the spire had not been sounded. Modern warfare with standing armies and mechanized gunfire tactics had rendered knighthood superfluous. The armor of the knights had come to be a fancy dress for tournaments, and the swords at their sides were part of their gentlemen's attire.

Yet among those who lived behind the heavy walls of the fortressed homes of Ávila, there were many whose hearts had remained bastions of the past. Theresa's father, the Castilian nobleman Don Alonso Sanchez de Cepeda, was one of them. In men like him the knightly fervor of faith, founded in a tradition of centuries, had preserved its ancient fighting spirit and assumed a hostile attitude toward those modern trends in which it recognized a new enemy, arising from within the ranks of Christianity itself.

Don Alonso was a man who lived as his forebears had lived, who clung tenaciously to their devout conception of honor, and ruled his house and brought up his children in accordance with the example which their austerity had set. He thought and judged and acted as his forebears had done, and he cherished the books, by which they too had been edified, the books of the saints and the chronicles of medieval heroes.

Theresa's mother, Doña Beatriz de Ahumeda, Don Alonso's young wife in second marriage, was of a different type. The routine of her life, her outward bearing, differed but little from that of her female forebears who, for centuries, had, fulfilled the duties of mothers and wives in the fortress homes of Ávila. But in her waking dreams this beautiful and lively woman left secretly the buttressed town and, freed of all domestic burden, traveled the seven seas, saw distant isles and lands, and lived through all sorts of worldly adventure. Her route through unknown realms was charted tor her by those fashionable novels which the printing presses, newly set up in Seville, turned out in profusion. Her guide was the "darkly beautiful" knight Amadis of Gaul, whom Cervantes was to dispose of a century later with the deadly weapon of his irony, but who at the time was guiding and misguiding man, an adventurous soul. The compiler of the Amadis novels, the Spanish alderman García Ordóñez de Montalvo, mastered the art of endlessly spinning out the adventures of his hero. Doña Beatriz, always ailing and more and more frequently confined to her bed, devoured the installments, as they appeared, with avid impatience.

Don Alonso, in his library, read himself up into heaven. Doña Beatriz, on her sickbed, read herself out into the world. In space the worlds of their dreams were as different as heaven and earth, but the time in which their souls felt at home was the same: the Middle Ages. Absorbed in the Flos Sanctorum devout Don Alonso looked up to the heaven of medieval sainthood, and the world through which Beatriz traveled, in pursuit of the adventures of Amadis, was by no means the world of the dawning century, which will of conquest and thirst of knowledge had begun to explore; it was a world filled with frightening and alluring adventures, dangers of travel, monsters of the sea, conflicts of love, exactly as it had been built up in the imagination of medieval minds.

Don Alonso observed the custom of his fathers when he read every night, for the edification of his family, from his stories of the saints. Doña Beatriz indulged merely her inclination when she told her children, in the absence of their father, about the newest feats of her admired hero.

The edifying stories of the father and the entertaining stories of the mother formed Theresa's awakening imagination to the same extent and marked her character with a certain ambivalence in which heavenly aspirations were combined with the interests of the world.

Theresa was a child of unusually strong imagination. She could transform her entire environment in accordance with her own world of fancy. The colonnaded patio, which was by tradition the center of all the activities of a Spanish household, had to comply with the quickly changing whims of the seven-year old girl, and became, in constant shifts of scenery, now the surging sea or distant land of fancy of Amadis of Gaul and now the field of battle, where pious knights fought valiantly against the infidels, or the hermitage and places of sacrifice of holy martyrs. And her playmates were crews or rulers or fighters for the faith, sea monsters, heathen barbarians or benevolent fairies.

Theresa's inexhaustible skill in inventing new games, her vivacity and boyish boldness, made her the natural leader of her numerous brothers and cousins. She was always the "darkly beautiful" knight, the victorious hero of the faith, the good fairy, or the saint who died a martyr's death, tied to a column in the court.

Until one day Theresa's childish fancy removed the last remaining barrier between reality and play . . . Then she decided to leave home secretly, together with her favorite brother Rodrigo, who was her elder by a few years, and to go to the land of the Moors—which, she was sure, lay somewhere outside the city gates of Ávila—to suffer at the hands of the ruler of the infidels the death of a martyr.

The two runaways succeeded in leaving the house unnoticed. They got outside the city walls and took the road to Salamanca. Dusk was falling, and the little feet were painfully dragging along. Theresa would not give up. In her imagination there was no distance that could not be covered. Just in back of the next bush, the white castle of the prince of the Moors would loom into view. But instead of the castle of her imagination the next bush brought the children surprisingly face to face with reality which came riding along on horseback in the guise of a cousin of their father's. He was on his way home from his fields which lay outside the city limits, and when he heard of the adventurous plan of the children, he reproved them severely and took them safely back to their worried parents.

After this unsuccessful venture Theresa invented a new game about nuns and monks as a substitute for "Spaniards and Moors," which had so far been her favorite game. The colonnade of the patio was the cloister. There was a chapel in the center of the court. On both sides were the cells in which the playmates were sitting, the nuns to the right, the monks to the left. They rejected all nourishment and prayed and were silent.

At the age of ten Theresa was a slender, somewhat awkward-looking girl, with deep black eyes and a serious expression which offset the friendly smile of her dimples in cheeks and chin. She had made a vow that she would actually become the nun whom she now pretended to be in her games, and that she would induce her brothers and cousins by her example to embrace likewise a spiritual life of world-abnegation.

At the age of fourteen, however, she was a precocious young lady and smiled condescendingly at the pious little thing she had been. Her boyishly slender body had lost its angular awkwardness and had developed the soft roundness of feminine forms. Her oily dark hair, her straight and almost reddish brows and her large pitch-black eyes, the seriousness of which seemed now hardly able to withstand the roguish mockery of her dimples, imparted to her youthful face a peculiar charm which it was hard to resist. Her inborn boldness had lost its boyishness and had developed into the quick and ready vivacity of a young girl whose beauty captivated everybody she met. When she laughed, and she liked to laugh and laughed often, her cheerfulness was of such springlike purity, that even the most sullen could not help chiming in.

At the age of seven Theresa had longed for a martyr's death, but at the age of fourteen she could not get too much of life, which meant to her to be courted and admired. At the age of ten she had chosen the nun's garb as an attire for the rest of her life, for she wanted to please God. Now she had no thought but to increase her beauty by finery and frills, for she wanted to please the world. She had a liking for orange and wore it whenever she could; for oranges had just been introduced in Europe and were still regarded as a luxury reserved for the fastidious taste of the few.

Her vivid imagination was applied now to the invention of ever new pranks and distractions. The patio was no longer a battleground for fighters of the faith; it had become the playground of handsome *caballeros*, true and real and not just the product of Theresa's wishful fancy. She had matured into womanhood and for a while her life pursued a normal course.

The strict Spanish etiquette, which tolerated no contact between young people of different sex unless they were relatives, was still in force at this time. But it had come to play more and more the role of a funny old chaperone whom the young in her charge managed to fool at every turn. All the handsome bachelor *caballeros* of Ávila discovered suddenly that they were somehow related to Theresa and vied with each other for the first dance with their beautiful "cousin," for a smile from her or for an encouraging glance.

The pious little girl had attained perfect mastery in the art of distributing promising looks to each and every contestant, until one day she met the "cousin" who was henceforth to have an exclusive claim to all her looks and all her smiles. This was the beginning of the first love of the much-courted young beauty, and it was quite in accord with the model of the times.

In the sixteenth century love had ceased to be merely a romantic dream of bliss. It had come to be an extremely real affair. The guardian angel of Theresa's first love was not a benevolent fairy but just an older cousin of a less well-to-do collateral line of the Cepeda family. This cousin knew more about life than Theresa and was well-versed in the business of love. Now she took charge of smuggling the first love letters of Theresa's admirer past Don Alonso's vigilance into his fortressed home. She delivered Theresa's replies and made arrangements for a secret rendezvous.

Strong walls and Don Alonso's old-time strictness guarded the Cepeda home against the aberrations of the coming age. And now the alien force of modern times made ready to sow its seed right in the soil of the Cepeda patio. Don Alonso's daughter was affected by the new spirit and in carefree exuberance and joy of life surrounded herself with a group of young people whom the splendors of worldliness held under their spell.

In the patio of the Cepedas the new century danced the lavolta, that same dance which the youth of Seville, drunk with life, danced at the golden gate. .In Don Alonso's home the new era frolicked and trifled, for it was tired of the solemnity of the past. A new generation flirted and dallied and was not worried by threats of hellfire and retribution. The faces of all these young beauties of Ávila glowed in the same unnatural crimson which the women of Seville applied to their cheeks when they went to the Golden Gate to welcome the ships returning with men and gold.

Teresa de Cepeda, the daughter of Don Alonso, was about to sell her virtue to the licentious new age, which had penetrated the inner court of the Cepeda stronghold in the guise of a relative and guest. But before the time arrived which the cousin had set for the first clandestine meeting, Theresa's strict training won the upper hand, and frightened by her own recklessness, she confessed everything to her father.

At this time Theresa's ailing mother was no longer alive. Don Alonso's eldest daughter María, who might have guided her young sister with motherly advice, was about to be married and had her own problems. There was no mature woman in the fortress home of the Cepedas, who could have helped a young girl to avoid all the dangers and pitfalls of the difficult years of adolescence. Don Alonso decided therefore to entrust the care of his daughter to the Augustinian nuns in Ávila. Their convent school was one of the few remaining institutions in which medieval discipline and rigor continued to prevail. Forty nuns were vigilantly guarding the wellbeing and virtue of the pupils attending their school.

The artificial crimson red was wiped from Theresa's face. Her orange-colored dresses were replaced by the plainest convent garb. The dance-trained grace of her gait had to be harnessed to the solemn measure of processions around the cloister. Instead of playful flirtations, there was to be prayer and devotion, and the edifying stories of the lady superior were the only substitute for the delightful little notes from the cousin and the gossipy stories of her friends. — At first Theresa felt deeply unhappy in her pious prison.

Her lively and spirited nature, however, could not go on forever in this mood of downhearted dejection, and before long she managed to make the best of what could not be changed. She learned to wear her plain convent garb with good grace. She no longer resented the solemn processions. She prayed as she was told to do. And she listened patiently to the edifying stories of the superior. The charm of her cheerful nature had not deserted her. It disarmed everyone around her and drew from the sternest face, from the most tightly closed lips, a friendly word or an encouraging smile.

After a few weeks Theresa was the favorite of the Augustinian nuns, she was a ray of light in the somber halls of the convent. And after the first year was over, as the days and weeks of the second year went by, when the end of her term in the convent approached and she was soon to return to the world, the good nuns made use of every kind of pious stratagem to induce Theresa to take the veil and stay with them.

But Theresa planned nothing of the sort. In all her docility she was only waiting for the moment when she might throw off the oppressive convent garb and slip back into a worldly dress and a worldly life. She longed and prayed for the day when the constant prayers would be over and she could take up again her uninterrupted life of an admired beauty with dance and flirtation.

"I was most averse to becoming a nun," she confessed at a later time and added that the mere thought of it had filled her with disgust. It was true, she had grown fond of the convent, but only as one may grow fond of a traveler's rest along one's road. Her home was out in the world, and all she intended to do right now was to be patient and wait until her apprenticeship was over and she could return to her life among people.

Then suddenly this life, which was about to become that of an average Spanish doña, was cut short, and the life of a saint continued in its stead. It did not begin in a flood of supernatural light, nor in heavenly elation, nor in joyous exuberance; it began in a *tremendum*, in "something to be trembled at;" it began in the darkness of night, in deadly weakness, in helpless moaning and unbearable pain.

Theresa had just completed her seventeenth year. Until then she had always been a healthy girl of even disposition. She was full of plans for a happy future, and since her days at the convent school were about to be over, she attended to her duties with redoubled zeal.

One day, in the midst of her usual routine, she was suddenly overwhelmed by illness. It began in a fit of unspeakable weakness; she could hardly keep on her feet. Then a piercing pain cut through her chest, spreading swiftly to the pit of her stomach, the neck and limbs, and finally through her entire body. She thought she must die then and there.

There she lay, a wretched creature, shaking with pain and trying desperately to escape its cruel clutches. Her face was flaming red; her breath came short and panting. The life in her body seemed to be ready to throw everything into a desperate final stand. Mumbled words, not articulated under conscious control, came from her mouth; then nothing but painful groans. The nuns were certain that the end had come.

But it was only a first attack. A few minutes later the pains subsided as suddenly and unexpectedly as they had come. The tenseness of her face was relaxed. Her eyes shone brightly. Her breath was quiet as before. Her cheeks had again their normal color. Theresa got up. She spoke as usual. She could take up again her daily routine, which the sudden seizure had interrupted.

On the surface everything followed again its normal course. But in her heart Theresa could find no rest. The memory of the awful experience haunted her. She was frightened by the mere thought that at any time and anywhere her forces might leave her again, that her body might again be turned into a bundle of pain, and that the world around her might again be severed from her senses. The light of day was no longer what it had been. It carried a lining of darkness. And over all her plans for future happiness and joy, there hovered the constant danger of a renewed attack.

Her fears were justified. After a while the attack did come again. And again and again. And every time it overwhelmed her with the same suddenness. Then Theresa knew that she had fallen victim to a malicious disease.

But precisely this dreadful illness was to be the first phase of her holiness. Her torment was the herald of undreamed-of bliss. Theresa had to suffer with the sick and the ailing before she could be one of God's elect.

Just as in the lower processes of nature violent tremors run through the earth to announce the beginning of volcanic upheavals; as the tide goes out before it comes in; as labors precede birth; so, in accordance with the same mysterious law, physical convulsions are often the beginning of spiritual upheavals that mark the start of higher form of existence; so is weakness the receding tide in the lives of men and announces the coining of the high tide of God; and so, in saintly and secular lives, sainthood and greatness are often born through the labors of pain and disease.

The great poet Novalis asked: "Is not illness often the beginning of the best in men?"

Like Theresa, the carefree and cheerful merchant's son Giovanni Bernadone was born by illness from his worldly entanglements and led on his way to become il Poverello, St. Francis of Assisi. The knight Iñigo de Oñez, whose life had been dedicated to the vanities of the world, recognized, in the course of his painful reconvalescence, that worldly ambitions are worthless and exchanged his secular aims for the heavenly aims of his new life through which he became St. Ignatius of Loyola.

Like Theresa, many a saint prepared himself in the utter darkness of a night of illness and pain for his journey along the shining road to heavenly glories. The Apostle Paul, who saw the Lord in a vision, bore his infirmities as a "thorn in the flesh." A sudden attack of illness had felled the persecutor of the Christians, Saul, on his way to Damascus. Then the Lord had appeared before him. Stricken with blindness he lay in his room in an inn by the roadside. And suddenly the light shone forth from within him, and the blind Saul became a seeing Paul.

St. Hildegard of Bingen, Theresa's great spiritual ancestor in the twelfth century, wrote once: "For almost a lifetime I struggled against the visions the Lord sent me, until finally the divine scourge forced me down on my sickbed. Then, urged by much suffering, I began to write, and as I proclaimed my vision, I regained my strength and arose from my bed."

For many a great prophet, reformer and founder of a new faith, pain and suffering were a great gift of divine grace. Mohammed, the prophet who conquered heaven for the infidels, suffered like Theresa throughout his entire life with the scourge of epileptic seizures. But what had begun as unbearable torture, was at last transformed into a blessing, and henceforth every new attack bestowed upon him new revelations and a new grace. A very similar story might be told about Cromwell, Luther, and many others.

In times, which conceived of greatness as greatness in faith, illness produced saints and prophets and founders of new faiths; but in times, in which greatness manifested itself in artistic or scientific achievements; the product of illness was equally often a man of genius in art or science. Pain became a tension which could be released in creative work, and the foreign matter of disease acted as a painful stimulant, not unlike the grain of sand which is introduced into the oyster and becomes the cause and center of a pearl.

For the poet Alfred de Musset illness meant inspiration, and Heine, who spent many years of his creative period as a living corpse in his "mattress-grave," praised it as the prime mover of all creation. The productive power of pain is manifest in the lives of a great number of creative men, and the biography of almost every genius is a treatise on the connection between suffering and achievement.

Pascal's immortal *Pensees* stand out against a dark background of never-ending ills. Behind the bars of his cell, between the most dreadful attacks and long lapses of deepest lethargy, Auguste Comte built up the marvelous structure of thought of his *Positive Philosophy.*

Vincent van Gogh wrote in a letter to his brother: "The more I fall to pieces, grow sicker and frailer, the more I become an artist; for through illness I get ideas for work in abundance." And indeed, in van Gogh's case illness was the irritant which made of the formally gifted copyist of Millet the greatest genius of modern painting.

An illness, quite similar to that in which Theresa's sainthood was rooted, gave Dostoevski the blessed power to produce his greatest works. In perusing the history of Dostoevski's illness and production, one might well mistake it for a story of Theresa's suffering and sainthood. "A strange and unbearable illness has always tortured me," writes Dostoevski. "I often felt that I must instantly die, and then something followed that was similar to real death: an attack which usually ended in a state of lethargy." Although Dostoevski suffered greatly with these attacks throughout his entire life, he knew about the creative force that was inherent in them and referred to them as his "sacred illness." "In such moments," he wrote, "I feel as though heaven had come down to earth to devour me. You men of good health, you cannot sense what feeling of bliss such illness can impart. For all the joys of life I would not give up the bliss of one such second."

When Theresa's condition failed to improve at school, Don Alonso took her home, for he hoped that, away frown the discipline of the convent, she would recuperate more quickly. The result he expected did not come about.

The fortress home, to which the patient returned, was no longer the same. Somber quiet weighed heavily on it. The spirited circle that had surrounded her in former years was no longer there. Most of her cousins, heeding the call of the times, had left Ávila. They worked for commercial houses in Seville or traveled in the wake of the conquistadors in distant lands. Of her brothers only the youngest two, Lorenzo and Antonio, had stayed at home. Most of her girlfriends were married and had followed their husbands to the big cities. Juana, her favorite, had stayed in Ávila, but, disillusioned with life, she had taken the veil.

At this time Theresa was just about sixteen years old. The looking glass would have shown her the same fascinating face as of old. With some powder and rouge and a smile she could have filled the patio in no time with a new set of courting caballeros and admiring friends. The interrupted frolic of her girlhood might have continued. But her happy look, her carefree smile had been chased away by her illness. There she stood, suffering and despondent, gazing vacantly into the court, which appeared to her as a dark and narrow prison yard. For the court continued to be what Theresa's imagination made of it.

At times she remembered the light and easy conversations of years gone by and saw herself again as the much-courted and spirited beauty. But a moment later her mind would dwell again on her present condition, and a wretched young girl, shaken by illness, was pacing forlornly up and down the prison yard.

The contrast between past and present made her the more pain fully aware of her pitiful state. The silence in the fortress house kept reminding her of how cruelly illness had deceived her in all her girlhood dreams and hopes. In her depressed moods, the sick girl fell the more readily victim to the attacks, which recurred now with ever increasing frequency.

Don Alonso was Theresa's only contact and not exactly the most suitable one. The secluded life which he led in his quiet and deserted house, had emphasized his introspective leanings. He spent his days almost completely in his library and devoted himself exclusively to his devotional books. Although he idolized his daughter, he could not, enthralled by stories of heroes and saints, find the way to the heart of a young girl, whose problem was simply that her life was shattered. The edification which he derived from his pious authors could not have been of help to his melancholy daughter. And when the attacks came, he faced them in helpless bewilderment.

He decided to entrust the girl to the care of his eldest daughter María, who lived on a little country estate in Castellanos. He hoped that the rural environment, together with María's loving care, might improve Theresa's state of health.

As soon as her condition permitted, Don Alonso put Theresa on a mule and started on the two-day trip. On the way they stopped in Hortigosa where Pedro de Cepeda, Don Alonso's elder brother, was living.

There, in one of the smallest rooms of his magnificent mansion, Theresa's uncle had lived for years the severely ascetic life of a man of God. Don Pedro was entirely concerned with life beyond the grave, his interest in the life here below had vanished completely, and when he spoke at all of the things of this world, he did so only insofar as they might serve him in his preparation for the great journey to God. His conversation with the unexpected guests was solely concerned with sacred things.

St. Jerome, the learned hermit of the fourth century, was Don Pedro's chosen model. From St. Jerome's admonitory writings he took the standard for all his acts. One of those heavy tomes he handed to his niece and asked her, for the edification of them all, to read a few passages which he had marked.

Theresa felt a certain resentment against these texts, which reminded her of her childhood, and it was at first out of sheer courtesy that she complied with her uncle's request. But while she was reading, her interest was aroused, and before long she listened to her own voice with the same devout attention as her audience. Now the voice which read St. Jerome's words was no longer the voice of monotonous boredom which it had been; it was a voice of pious concentration. A frightened and suffering young girl was reading the message of the kingdom of heaven as a message of solace for the sick and ailing. And when they left the following day, Theresa requested from her uncle a volume of Jerome's writings, which she wished to take with her on her trip to the country.

At first the rural environment did not seem to bring about the hoped-for recovery. Neither the tender care of her half-sister nor the distractions of country life could restore her cheerful disposition. The comforting words of her relatives tormented her, and she was happy only when she was left alone in her room, absorbed in her volume of St. Jerome. His words of promise about the kingdom of heaven, addressed to all those who strove here below to lead a life pleasing to God, revived in her the old dream of becoming a nun. Her former love of life and worldliness, however, was not altogether dead; it was only ailing; and as soon as there was the faintest hope for recovery, it put in its claims against the intimidated patient who was ready to seek refuge in a convent.

Then one day Theresa came in her readings across St. Jerome's threats of hellfire and punishment. All the things which her frustrated hunger for life had been craving—the desire to be admired, flirtations, secret love affairs, even the most harmless excesses in dress and make-up, all these things were enumerated there and condemned one by one as infallible guides to hell. And if St. Jerome's rhetoric had been impressive when he described with mellow tenderness what joys the heavens could promise to those who turned their backs on the world, it was even more so, when he began with scolding fury to describe the hellish torment awaiting those, who had devoted their lives to the concerns of the world. Theresa was frightened to the quick.

A short time later she suffered another severe attack. María spent the night by her bedside. She lay there in a coma, and her sister was ready to despair.

The following morning Theresa left her room and to every body's surprise was a changed person. As though her illness had vanished without a trace she made again the impression of a care free young girl. Nobody understood the reason for this sudden transformation. Theresa herself explained at a much later time that St. Jerome's threats of retribution in hell had done for her what his promises of heavenly joy had not been able to do. Fear of hell induced the wavering girl to choose between heavenly and worldly joys. She chose to turn her back on the world and start on her road to heaven. Once she had resolved to become a nun, her pain and her suffering left her. It was as though the "little deaths" of her illness had only been meant to serve as a poignant reminder of the imminence of the dangers of hell. Her melancholy which had cast a shadow on her soul had disappeared too. The heavenly light, toward which she was now moving, knew of no shadows. And pain and illness, life and death, everything was transfigured in its radiance.

Once before Theresa had been planning to become a nun, but afterwards, when she had grown conscious of her beauty and charm, she had rejected the idea as childish and ridiculous. Now, however, when illness had taught her about the transitoriness of the glories of the world, when the threats of hell had filled her soul with unspeakable horror, nothing could make her desist from her vow.

For fear that her plan might again be thwarted, she kept it a strict secret. After her return to Ávila she took only her intimate friend Juana into her confidence, for Juana was a nun herself and would be able to help her attain her end.

Not to attract the attention of the devil, who is lurking everywhere in the world, who is lurking in the advice of friends as well as in the doubting minds of well-meaning relatives, Theresa employed a pious stratagem. That nobody might suspect her intentions, she participated in social activities and talked and smiled and flirted as in the olden days. But she was firmly resolved to bid the world farewell. Once a *caballero* expressed in no uncertain terms his admiration for her shapely legs, and she retorted in a quick come-back: "Look well, it may be your last chance!" Everyone laughed and assumed that she thought of marriage, and that her remark was an allusion to the imminence of her union with another wooer. At that time, however, she had already completed her preparations for donning the modest garb of the brides of Christ.

As soon as Juana had finished the necessary arrangements, so that Theresa would merely have to appear at the Carmelite convent of the Incarnation to be received there as a novice, she decided to inform her father of what she intended to do.

Don Alonso was thunderstruck. To be sure, he was a good Christian. He admired the saints and martyrs, and their lives of sacrifice inspired and edified him. But then he was also a father, who was attached to his child in earthly love. The Christian and the father came into conflict, and the father won and protested vehemently against Theresa's plan. Don Alonso was on good terms with his God. He gave Him everything he owed Him and more, but it was not possible that the Lord should demand the sacrifice of his daughter.

Theresa had always been an obedient daughter, but hell was a serious matter, and Don Alonso's strictest orders could not induce her to abandon her plan. To escape her father's vigilance she did now, at the age of seventeen, what she had done once before when she was seven. She ran away. Then she had persuaded her brother Rodrigo to flee with her to the land of the Moors, and now she took her youngest brother Antonio with her on her flight from the world.

Early one morning Antonio and Theresa left the fortress house. They separated at the gate of the monastery of St. Thomas where the Grand Inquisitor Torquemada lies buried. Antonio entered and asked the Dominican friars to admit him as a novice. Theresa went on to the Carmelite convent of the Incarnation, a few miles away from the town, where her friend Juana was expecting her.

Antonio's plan failed as soon as he had crossed the threshold of the monastery. It was at St. Thomas that Don Alonso went to confession, and the Dominicans were cautious enough to send word to him to inquire whether Antonio's decision met with his approval. A short while later Don Alonso appeared at the monastery and took his runaway son back to his home.

Thanks to Juana's forethought and skill, Theresa's plan was much better prepared. Don Alonso was notified of his daughter's move too, but he arrived at the convent only in time to see how Theresa's beautiful curls were cut off and how she exchanged her worldly dress of orange color for the white veil of the Carmelite novice. He was faced with an accomplished fact, and all he could do was to give his belated blessing.

At the Carmelite convent of the Incarnation, isolated from the world by heavy walls, Theresa believed herself safe from all temptations. "I was filled with the greatest of joys," she wrote at a later time about her entrance into the convent, "and God converted the acidity of my embittered soul into the greatest tenderness." She was zealous and cheerful in the fulfillment of her duties as a novice. Obedience to her meant liberation; her cell was a real home; and renunciation filled her with consummate joy.

The initial happiness of her novitiate, however, did not last. The fear of hell which had driven her to take the veil, and the zeal with which she pursued her road to heaven sharpened her eyes for what was going on around her. To her great dismay she found that the place to which she had fled lay still in the world from which she had meant to escape.

The chief enemy was the changed spirit of the times. To be sure, the walls of the Incarnation were thick and high, but they separated the convent from the world outside only in space, not in time. And then as now, time meant change; it meant change of things and of thoughts; it was an all-pervading, all-embracing power. Within and without the Incarnation, time had changed from the Middle Ages to Modern Times. No wall and no rampart could shut out time. There was no place beyond its reach. Nobody could escape it. The busy life of the world and the life of contemplation in the convent, distraction and renunciation occurred in the same century, were keyed to the same tenor of life.

The walls of the Incarnation were medieval, but those who lived behind them were children of modern times. The veil belonged to the Middle Ages, but the women who wore it were of the sixteenth century. The prayers, masses, devotions, observances, all the elements of the routine regulating the daily life of the Carmelites, came out of medieval times; but the life thus regulated was the life of nuns in the year 1536. The spirit of the Middle Ages had dictated the forms of prayer, medieval music had composed the hymns of the choir. But those who prayed the prayers and sang the songs were nuns of a modern era.

The little chapel with its leaking roof, through which the rain could drip down on the heads and shoulders of the praying nuns, kept faith with the old vow of poverty and abnegation. But in the cells of the Incarnation, which were really little two-room apartments, the sisters knew how to live a life of renunciation with ease and in comfort. They owned nothing, but they accepted little favors. Their robes were mended, but they wore necklaces, bracelets and rings. Before God they were all equal as brides of Christ, but those of noble birth retained the title of "Doña." The meals were made to conform with all the prescribed fasts, but they were appetizing and ample, and in between the nuns had all sorts of titbits and dainties.

The pious sisters served the Lord in chastity and obedience, but from time to time they had their day out or even a long vacation which they could spend as they pleased with relatives or friends out in the world.

And just as the inmates of the convent could go to see the world, so the world could come to visit the convent. Seclusion from the world was no longer a genuine withdrawal from the world but rather a game of hide and seek. The home of the silent Carmelites had opened its doors to the modern cult of talk and conversation. One of the rooms of the Incarnation had been sublet to the world. Upstairs were the cells, and just a few steps led down to the parlor below where the nuns could receive guests of both sexes. To be sure, there was in the *locatorio* a metal grate which separated the nuns from their worldly callers, but it was a partition which separated only the bodies in space and could be crossed by sight and hearing. Through it the silence of the convent and busy worldliness, renunciation and greed could engage in amicable conversation. And in the restless mirror of gossip the world was reflected with all its vanities and temptations.

In her quiet cell Theresa conversed with God and felt secure. But whenever she had to appear in the parlor, she found herself confronted with the world she had meant to flee. Soon she came to recognize that her heart too was such a convent with cells and devotion upstairs and a parlor one flight below. Her peace of mind was gone. She saw that she was still within the range of the powers of hell.

In such moments she began to doubt the wisdom of her selection of the Carmelite Incarnation as a homestead for her religious life. And these doubts in her mind were the first indication that the great reformer of the order of the Carmelites that Theresa was destined to become at a later time was beginning to stir in her. For the moment, however, she was only a little novice whose duty it was to be humble and to obey. The concessions which the Carmelite order made to the ways of the world had been sanctioned by the Pope in the so-called mitigated rule, and a little novice could not be more papal than the Pope. What happened in the Incarnation, was the consecrated custom of the times, and all the sisters, from the prioress down, paid homage to it. The force of convention smothered Theresa's doubts, and it is probable that she would have submitted to the established routine, that her life would have become that of the average Spanish nun of her day, if illness had not intervened for the second time and had pulled her out of the rut of the accepted system.

After she had taken her vows as a nun, her former attacks came back with increased violence. They overcame her with the relentless fury of elemental events. No part of her body remained unaffected; no function stayed immune; no limb, no muscle, no nerve was safe from the blazing pain. And the agony of her "little deaths" resembled ever more the real agony of the great death.

The frightened nuns called her by her name. She remained motionless. They shook her, rubbed her, lifted her up. All their efforts were in vain. Her body remained cold and rigid as though she had died.

As the attacks recurred, the illness extended its hold over Theresa's entire life. Some of her organs were never entirely free from pain. And from one attack to the next the respite granted her grew shorter and shorter. At first it was a matter of weeks but finally only of days.

Theresa faced these visitations in helpless despair. Once she had heeded the exhortation which her illness seemed to convey. She had left the world and had gone into the convent; but for a second time, and with increased brutality, it barred her way, thwarted her plans, and threw her out of the quiet ease of convent routine.

Theresa was destined to achieve greater things. She was to become the saint of ecstasy, and her illness was a contributing factor in the development of her sainthood. But as yet this sainthood, maturing under the veil of pain, was invisible to profane eyes.

Don Alonso took his daughter out of the convent and called the best Castilian physicians to her bedside. They came, solemnly dressed in their gowns and caps, Galen's writings in one hand and the indispensable urinal in the other. In keeping with the prevailing methods of diagnosis, they felt the pulse and examined the urine with learned pedantry. Then they proceeded to consult their authority Galen and vied with each other in theoretical discussions about the cause of the patient's condition. But with all their protracted talk they could find no organic defect, and their theoretical conclusions and deductions failed to explain the fainting spells, the twitching of muscles, the convulsions and the tonic rigidity which characterized Theresa's case.. It was clearly a case not provided for in the handbooks of medicine, and the prescriptions, which the doctors' syllogistic rationale seemed to call for, remained ineffective.

Since science had failed so pitifully, Don Alonso decided to entrust the treatment of his daughter to a lay healer, a so-called *curandera*. The one in Becedas whom he consulted enjoyed the reputation of having cured innumerable hopeless cases. She was a sort of naturopath and practiced only in spring when the herbs began to sprout. It was now the beginning of winter, and so it was decided that Theresa should spend the intervening months with her sister María in the country. The trip was again interrupted in Hortigosa, and again the short stay at Don Pedro's brought about a decisive turn in Theresa's development. It was one of those little coincidences which always seem to play into the hand of a greater necessity.

This time the pious uncle gave his ailing niece a book by a Franciscan monk, the

Spaniard Francisco de Osuna. She meant to read it on her journey to Castellanos, but it came to be her guide on her journey to God. Its title was *The Third Abecedarium*, and instead of the verbal prayer which had become a formal routine, it taught an unspoken spiritual form of prayer. "God is without speech, He is the essence of quiet," taught this mystic disciple of St. Francis, "and only those who approach Him in silence can be heard and will be given an answer." It was a sort of spiritual A B C of a silent language, which Osuna called the mother tongue of heaven.

When, during her stay in the country, the attacks slackened at times, Theresa practiced the mystical A B C, and the same joyous excitement overcame her which children experience when they learn how to spell out the letters in their first primer. And her delight was truly that of a child who is about to master the rudiments of spelling and senses vaguely that the letters fall into words and phrases which have meaning and coherence, that they are the key to a world which one may enter by dint of assiduous practice. Her mouth, used to the spoken word, was not as yet able to pray in silence and to call God by his wordless name. Her untrained ear could not as yet understand the unworded language of the Lord. Nor had her eye as yet acquired the ability to see what is not seeable. The first ray of light which emanated for her from Osuna's book was merely a flicker in the darkness of her sickroom; for in the life of Theresa, illness was still stronger than sainthood.

When spring came, Theresa traveled to Becedas. The cure was a sort of medieval shock therapy and consisted mainly in drastic attempts to stir up the entire organism. All sorts of herbs, vomitives and purgatives were used to clean out the body. But since the *curandera* thought of the disease as an evil demon who had settled down in the patient, she added to her natural expellents all kinds of exorcistic concoctions, which she prepared, by means of magical formulae, from the toes of spring frogs, pulverized wings of the first flies and fresh excreta of snakes.

The demon of Theresa's illness not only failed to be intimidated by all the sorcery of the *curandera*; he actually redoubled his opposition and seemed to resent the witch's unauthorized intervention in his own private affairs. The cure of the *curandera* proved more disastrous than the illness itself.

"I do not know how I ever stood it," Theresa wrote in her autobiography. "I remained three months in that place, in the most grievous sufferings. In two months my life was nearly worn out, and the severity of the pain in my heart, for the cure of which I was there, was much more keen; it seemed to me now and then as if my heart had been seized by sharp teeth. There was a great loss of strength, for an excessive disgust for food did not allow me to take anything except liquids. The fever never left me and increased during the treatment. It seemed to me that a fiery conflagration was consuming me from within. My sinews began to shrink. The pains I had were unendurable, and I was so overwhelmed by the deepest sadness that I had no rest either night or day. All in all this cure left in me but a faint breath of life."

When Theresa's father took her home again to Ávila in the summer of 1537 it was a human wreck that moved into the fortress house of the Cepedas. Theresa yearned for death as the only deliverance from her torment and asked to make her confession.

Superstitious love induced Don Alonso to deny her request. He feared that such a confession, conceived as a preparation for death, might in some magic way accelerate death itself.

Deprived of the last consolation, which the sacrament could have given her, the patient got into a state of excitement which neither body nor soul could endure for long. In the same night she suffered an attack which surpassed in fury everything she had experienced before. Her convulsions became a delirium of pain. She raged against herself. Her nails cut deep into her flesh. She screamed in anguish. She bit her tongue. The death rattle broke from her bluish lips. But the horrible torment continued until finally she fell into a coma in which she lay cold and motionless as though she had finally been relieved of all human suffering.

A night and a day passed, and still there was not the slightest sign of life in her prostrate body. The doctors tried to take her pulse but could not feel it. The hand they held was lifeless and icy. The mirror they placed before her mouth remained undimmed by the breath of life. "She is dead!" they said, and for them the case was closed.

"My daughter is not dead!" cried Don Alonso as though he had lost his mind. It was not possible that God should punish him so harshly.

A second night went by and Theresa had not yet recovered. It was high time to begin preparations for the funeral. The body must be washed. It must be wrapped in winding sheets, and candles must be lighted, right and left, at the head of the bier.

Two sisters of the Incarnation prayed and kept the watch. The following morning the nuns dug Theresa's grave in the cemetery of the convent. In the chapel a mass was read for the soul of the deceased, and the sisters sang solemn funeral hymns.

In the afternoon the prioress of the Incarnation appeared at Don Alonso's home to have Theresa's body transferred to the convent. With the stubbornness of a loving father Don Alonso refused to admit her to the bier. "My daughter is not dead!" he cried even now, when the body was ready to be interred. Pain and grief seemed to have robbed him of his senses. The prioress had to leave without effecting her purpose.

The following night, the third since the attack, Theresa's younger brother kept the watch. Toward morning he was overcome by sleep. When he awoke, he saw that the bier stood in flames. One of the candles had burned down and had fallen on the winding sheet. In a panic he called in the servants who managed to put out the fire. Thus Theresa was saved from burning to death.

For a day and a half Theresa's grave had been ready in the cemetery of the convent. All preparations for the interment were complete. The sisters were angered by this unseemly delay, and for a second time the prioress went to Don Alonso's home to demand the body which belonged to the convent. She resolutely entered the death chamber and, to her amazement, found Theresa, whom she had thought dead and ready to be buried, calmly sitting on her bier. On her lids were still the drops of wax, which had fallen down from the melting candles, but she was speaking to Don Alonso in a clear and natural tone of voice, imploring him to let her make her confession. It was as though she were just finishing the sentence which the attack had cut short, as though the four-day period of absolute lifelessness had not intervened at all. Now the prioress, who had come to claim the dead body of one of her nuns, could do nothing but fulfill the wishes of her who had just returned to life and go to call for her father confessor.

After Theresa had made her confession and had partaken of the sacrament, she felt relieved in her soul. Her physical infirmity, however, remained unchanged. In her autobiography she gives a vivid description of the devastating effects which this latest attack had wrought: "After those four days, during which I was insensible, so great was my distress, that our Lord alone knows the intolerable suffering I endured. My tongue was bitten to pieces; there was a choking in my throat because I had taken nothing, and because of my weakness, so that I could not swallow even a drop of water; all of my joints seemed to be out of joint, and the disorder of my head seemed extreme. I was bent together like a coil of ropes—for to this was I brought by the torture of those days—unable to move either arm or foot, or hand, or head, any more than if I had been dead, unless others moved me—I could raise, I think, one finger of my right hand. As to touching me, that was impossible, for I was so bruised that I could not endure it. They used to move me in a sheet, one holding one end and one the other."

In this state, in accordance with her wishes, she was taken back to the convent on Palm Sunday of the year 1537. "There," she relates, "they received one whom they had waited for as dead; but her body was worse than dead . . . It is impossible to describe my extreme weakness, for I was nothing but bones."

For eight months Theresa lay in the infirmary of the convent, totally paralyzed and tortured by unrelenting pains. Finally, when the seizure subsided somewhat, when she could at least manage to drag herself about, she was moved back to her cell, where she spent three more years in a state of partial paralysis and severe contractures. There were no signs of improvement. For three years she led the life of an invalid.

Finally Theresa did free herself from the laming grip of her disease, but even then she continued to suffer with all sorts of other ailments and ills. "So weak was my stomach," she writes, "that for twenty years I could not keep any food until late in the afternoon. The times when I was not harassed by various severe pains were rare, indeed."

Modern physicians would hold the backwardness of scholastic medicine responsible for the fact that their sixteenth-century colleagues viewed Theresa's illness as an inexplicable mystery. At that time doctors had no very exact knowledge of the structure of the organism; they knew nothing about hormones; they were not equipped with brain-wave detectors, cardiographs, X rays, metabolic recorders and all the other diagnostic helps, which make it possible for modern medicine to track down the most hidden diseases.

But even supposing that none of these means could yield the desired result in the case of an illness like that of Theresa, modern medicine would still not be ready to admit defeat. For when a pathological phenomenon cannot be traced to a physiological cause, the case can still be referred to the science of psychiatry, which may find that a psychic disturbance is responsible for the organic complaint. There are on record in the clinical experience of modern psychiatry a considerable number of cases in which certain states of consciousness or of psychic excitement have caused anatomic or functional changes in tissues and organs.

Our contemporary science would summarize the symptoms of Theresa's illness about as follows: her convulsions were tonic contractions; the rigidity of her muscles was a form of muscular tetanization; the choking sensation, which made it so difficult for her to swallow, was a *globus hystericus*; her unendurable pain is indicative of hyperesthesia; her frequent fainting spells were due to nervous disorders in the circulatory system; and her entire illness, which stayed with her from adolescence to mature womanhood, was a classical example of those psycho-physiological disturbances which can at times be observed in women between puberty and menopause. In the final diagnosis there might at best be some disagreement as to whether Theresa's case was straight hysteria or hystero-epilepsy. As for the best possible treatment, there would be no doubt either. It would consist in a cold-water cure with luminal and dilatin as drugs and possibly psychoanalysis.

Yet the most painstaking medical analysis would miss the point. It would label a disease but not the phenomenon behind it. This belongs to a sphere outside the province of medical science. What becomes manifest in the life of St. Theresa, is the interdependence of illness and creative greatness. Hers is one of the cases in which the term illness as such cannot explain anything. The pathological phenomenon merely deepens the miracle. And a mere pathography of St. Theresa is just as inadequate, when taken as an attempt to define her true nature, as all the pathographies which try to explain the greatness of St. Paul, of Luther, Mohammed or Dostoevski in exclusively medical terms.

A really great modern physician, Carl Ludwig Schleich, whose name is not only linked with his epochal achievements in psychiatry but who is famous for his discovery of spinal anesthesia, is among the rare scientists of modern times who have come to recognize that medical nomenclature cannot do justice to the phenomena hidden beneath the symptoms of hysteria. To him hysteria is merely a symbolic expression for something that is otherwise not observable in nature. In his opinion hysteria signifies that the spirit has gained mastery over matter, that it is trying to form an organism after its own image. At the basis of the phenomena to which we apply the term of hysteria, there is a complex of ideas which is conceived in the spirit but acts in the body. The real essence of this illness can be understood, according to Schleich, only on the basis of the metaphysical principle which underlies all of creation. The world with its manifold forms was created after the pattern of one plastic idea. And that is precisely what can be seen in hysteria, through a powerful microscope, as it were, which permits us to study life and growth in nature somewhat more closely than the naked eye and a so-called healthy common sense are capable of doing.

If one examines Theresa's illness carefully, it becomes unmistakably clear that a higher principle is active in it, and this to such an extent that illness and sainthood appear at times merely as two different manifestations of one and the same creative force.

Theresa's vita represents thus a very peculiar type of saintly existence, in which suffering plays into the hand of greatness, in which the patient gives the cue to the saint. The cutting pains which sever her from a worldly enjoyment of life, guide her thoughts in the direction of heavenly bliss, and the more often her personal will is eliminated in spells of physical fainting, the more readily does it make way for guidance by the superpersonal will of God.

But the function of illness in Theresa's case is not exhausted in purification and change of life. It made all her senses and her entire body more receptive, more sensitive and ready for supersensual experiences. Her illness effected a breach in the bodily ramparts of her existence, and through it higher forces were able to move in. "Sometimes," she writes, "a feeling of the presence of God would come over me, unexpectedly, so that I could in no wise doubt either that He was within me, or that I was wholly absorbed by Him." This sensation came to be more and more the decisive force in Theresa's life and finally culminated in that state of rapturous enchantment which no created being can attain by purely created means. For this state of existence lies outside the realm of the senses. In it Theresa saw what no eye can see; she heard what no ear can hear; and she understood what no mind can fathom.

In her *Interior Castle* Theresa wrote about these things: "One feels that one has been wholly transported into another and a very different region from that in which we live, where a light so unearthly is shown that if during one's whole lifetime one would be trying to picture it and the wonders seen, one should not possibly be able to succeed. In an instant the mind learns so many things at once that if the imagination and the intellect spent years in striving to enumerate them, they could not recall a thousandth part of them."

Trying to describe these raptures Theresa says that in them "an upward flight takes place in the interior of the soul, and this with the swiftness of a bullet fired from a gun." And in these states such superiority is at times given to the inner forces over those without, to the soul over its body, to heaven over earth, that the laws of nature are suspended, that the earth waives its right to gravity, that, when the soul starts its flight to heaven, the body is weightlessly raised from the ground. Extraordinary events in the soul are coupled with extraordinary events in matter; ecstasy is complemented by levitation.

What happens here, is a thing not within nature. The continuity of the physical world is disrupted. Time is dissolved in eternity, and nature makes way for the supernatural. Yet all this occurs within the realm of created space and time. A Carmelite nun of the sixteenth century, in the convent of the Incarnation at Ávila, is carried away to heaven, while her body hovers above the ground. The paradox becomes fact. Human existence becomes divine. Illness supplies the tangible dynamics. Illness is the abyss of suffering and death, over which nature achieves its leap into the supernatural.

When the disease suspends all functions of organic life, an interregnum ensues, which gives rise to a new form of existence. It is the existence of ecstasy and is equipped with supernatural powers. When the eyes of the body are blinded to the light of created nature, because the impact of illness has closed the lids over them, then a new eye is opened, which is able to perceive the radiance of God. When illness deafens the physical ear, the soul itself becomes capable of perceiving the inaudible words which the voice of the Creator speaks. When unconsciousness veils the mirrors of physical perception, the ultimate essence of things appears unmirrored and unmattered. When reason is brought to naught by the onslaught of physical illness, then revelation can begin to speak truths which exceed reason. When the heart ceases to beat in the rhythms of this world, then a new heart arises that beats in the rhythms of God.

The suddenness of Theresa's seizures, with their abrupt shifts from life to lifelessness, trained her body for the higher shifts from natural existence to supernatural ecstasies. Resurrection from death, the miracle of all myths, the sequence of lowly dying and higher life, were given the reality of historical truth. Out of the "little deaths" of a Spanish nun was born St. Theresa, the saint of ecstasy.

Theresa was about seventeen years old when she was overcome by the first attack of her illness. She was forty-three, when she was granted her first ecstatic rapture. She had passed through numberless "little deaths" before finally sainthood could crystallize out of illness, rapturous bliss out of physical torment.

During these twenty-five years of almost continuous suffering and pain, her saintliness was merely a little spark which flickered through the darkness of an interminable night. Even when it finally blazed forth in a brighter flame, its light kept a dark lining as a vestige of the disease from which it had sprung. Her ecstatic raptures displayed all the symptoms of her morbid attacks and differed from them only in that they occurred in supernatural spheres. Eyewitness accounts, as that of the sister sacrist of Toledo, point out that in her ecstasies Theresa had no control over her senses, that her pulse stopped beating, that her breath was suspended, that her entire body was so rigid that it could not be moved, and that her hands and feet were cold as though she had died.

Almost her entire life consisted of days of suffering, of nights of pain and death-like lethargies. In the beginning she sought the help of men in her struggle against the disease. But after a time she abandoned the medicines of the doctors and relied on the "medicine of saints," which does not attempt to remove the disease but teaches how to endure it.

The example of the Biblical sufferer, and still more the words of Christ from the Gospel according to St. Matthew, "And he that taketh not his cross and followeth after me is not worthy of me," were the source of her strength and made it finally possible that her suffering lost its sting and her illness its power to frighten. She recognized that they were part of her fate and accepted them humbly.

The really great danger in Theresa's life was not lurking in the sickroom but in the parlor. Not pains but distractions obstructed her path to sainthood. Not illness but recovery, which opened the doors of the sickroom and confronted her with the decisive problem: the world.

It came to pass in the year 1540.

Theresa recovered from one day to the next after the doctors had given up her case as incurable. One morning she awoke and found that her limbs were no longer paralyzed. She was able to get up and walk as before. She herself ascribed this unhoped-for recovery to the force of prayer, and there are modern scientists, as for instance Alexis Carrell, who agree that concentrated prayer can accumulate curative energies, which affect the organism in such a way that functional disturbances and anatomical defects are removed. The nuns of the Incarnation, who had left Theresa the day before as an invalid in her cell, thought it a miracle of God, when they saw her walking freely toward them.

Theresa was given back to the life of the convent; she could attend to her duties as a nun; she could take part in communal devotions; she could sing in the choir and visit the parlor. She returned, surrounded by the halo of one on whom a miracle had been performed. Everybody remembered the Palm Sunday three years ago, when Theresa, whom the doctors had pronounced dead, came back to life and was carried in a sheet through the streets of Ávila to the convent of the Incarnation. Throughout the time of her total paralysis, the whole town had taken an active interest in the pitiful fate of the incurable nun. And now she could be seen again behind the grate of the parlor, moving about like all the others, thanks to the power of prayer. A miracle had happened in the convent of the Incarnation. Every visitor could see it with his own eyes, could hear how it had all come about from the lips of Theresa herself.

It seems but natural that the whole town came streaming to the convent. They all came, relatives and friends, the faithful who wished to find confirmation of their faith, the curious, and the skeptics who hoped to unmask a pious fraud. At the gates of the Incarnation, long rows of callers were patiently waiting their turn.

The prioress was not slow in recognizing the great advantages which might accrue for the Incarnation from this-unexpected turn of events. Theresa was a living example of the power of faith. The convent of the Carmelites was poor, and if God had chosen it as the scene of His miracle, He obviously meant to distinguish it by a special token of His grace. In an age when the wealthy preferred to invest their money in commerce and trade, only an extraordinary occurrence could induce them to be liberal with charitable gifts. So Theresa was encouraged and even ordered to appear frequently in the parlor, even though it might be to the detriment of her devotional exercises. This pious calculation was correct. Theresa became a sacred exhibit, an important source of revenue for the Incarnation.

She attended to her new duties with ready obedience and even in a spirit of satisfied complacency. Yet the doubts, which, during the time of her novitiate, had been troubling her, came to the fore again too, warning her with ever increased insistence that the world was again laying a snare for her. For in the parlor she was surrounded by people who marveled only at the visible miracle of her recovery, without suspecting anything about the much greater invisible miracle of the mystic visions which could not be removed from the solitude and quiet of her cell.

Her inner experience of saintliness was forced to compete with her existence in the parlor; the indescribable, invisible mystic miracle, known to God alone, was forced to rival the describable and demonstrable miracle of her recovery. It was apparent that the mystic nun in her quiet cell would sooner or later come into conflict with the convent attraction exhibited in the parlor. It was an external factor, a devilish trick of fate, which brought the situation to a head.

The force that brought the people of Ávila ever again to the parlor of the Incarnation, attracting them with never-waning fascination, was Theresa's natural beauty, which her illness had only served to increase. Her delicate smile, in which a twenty-two year-old girl and an angel seemed to be smiling together, her ethereal charm, and the magic of her words, in which the worldly intelligence of a human being was coupled with the supernatural experience of a soul who had tasted death, were the delights of al visitors. There was, in all this, an element of piquancy which made of the convent parlor a rendezvous of Ávila's social life with Theresa as its center.

But her beauty was not to go scot free. Who pleases will sense the pleasure of pleasing. At first Theresa had gone to the parlor in a spirit of devout obedience. But after a while she stayed there because she found it hard to resist the delight of being admired. In the parlor she was a servant of the world, not only in compliant with her vow of obedience but also for the sake of her own enjoy meat. And just then the world with all its happenings, manifestations and experiences presented the sharpest contrast to what was revealed to Theresa in the seclusion of her cell. Never before had the art of conversation been so exclusively concerned with the things of the earth. Never had it been so exclusively determined by the confusion and evanescence of earthly phenomena. Hardly a day passed without surprising events. The people lived in a constant tension, and the rhythm of their talk was patterned after the tempo of their lives. At one moment the news of the discovery of a new cosmic law filled the intellect with amazed admiration, but a moment later it was the report that a ship with a cargo of gold had arrived in Seville, which excited the imagination. Now people were thrilled by a new mystic poem dealing with the passion of Christ, and immediately thereafter they were equally enthusiastic about an orange which a visitor had brought along and passed around in the parlor as a dainty curiosity. A minute ago these men and women had listened with bated breath to the most recent verdict of the Inquisition, and now they concentrated their amused interest on the latest gossip about town. Reports on adventures in distant lands, the revived problem of Platonic love and the debut of a sportive *gracioso* in some new comedy were eagerly discussed as equally fascinating topics of the day. The conversation of these men and women, just, as their lives, shifted from one theme to the next, without rhyme or reason, without continuity or perseverance. The forms of social discourse which have survived to the present day were developed in the sixteenth century. It was Theresa's time which cultivated the light and easy touch and pass of superficial conversation, the quick and witty thrust and repartee, that form of dialog which was no longer meant to clarify, to edify, but merely to give and find distraction in the multifariousness of, life.

Yet the spiritual prayer which Theresa practiced in her cell, demanded contemplation of God in concentration upon the one and only essence.

As Theresa's mystic visions increased in frequency, it became ever more apparent that it is not just a difference in degree which separates one whom God has chosen from one who basks in the admiration of a motley group of worldly socialites. Only a flight of stairs separated Theresa's cell from the parlor. Every day Theresa descended this flight of stairs. But from day to day, from time to time, the distance grew. It continued to grow until it became the abyss which separates heaven from earth. In her cell Theresa sat as an angel in heaven conversing with God in silent prayer her descent to the parlor was the fall of an angel. As a fallen angel she listened eagerly to the news of the world and participated in the frivolous gossip in the parlor of the convent.

God did not want to lose his nun, and He was very patient. When Theresa returned to the quiet of her cell, the door which led to heaven was always open. Every time she promised herself never again to go down to the parlor. But when the convent clock struck the hour of worldliness, the nun obeyed its call.

Unwillingly and willingly, unconsciously and consciously, she was guiltless and guilty to the same degree. Her talents and temperament made her excel in conversation. She liked to ask and liked to listen. Her answers were quick and ready. She mastered the art of singling out the salient point and could tell a good story to everybody's delight. She was charming and was charmed herself. She was be loved and loved people herself. The more often she came to the parlor, the more she succumbed to the ways of the world. She had fallen a prey to the vanity of words.

When she realized to what dangers her higher aspirations had come to be exposed, she was frightened and tried to escape. But she failed miserably. "On the one hand," she writes, "God was calling me, on the other I was following the world. I wanted to combine these two opposites: spiritual life with its delights and the life of the senses with its pleasures." And when she recognized that these two opposites were not compatible with each other, she decided in favor of—the world.

Theresa who had remained steadfast in torture and pain, whom no illness had been able to deter in the pursuit of her holy ends hoisted the flag of surrender before the vain distractions of the world. Her spiritual prayer, her communion with God, the quiet of contemplation, the mystic visions, everything the Lord had given her she now decided to sacrifice to the world.

Desperate helplessness together with pious humility were responsible for this amazing decision. "My soul," she writes, "was then so distracted by many vanities that I was ashamed to draw near unto God in any act of such special friendship as that of mental prayer." Her decision was a sort of self-inflicted punishment. The saint deprived the nun of the gift of grace.

Theresa abandoned the prayer of silence. God appeared no longer in her cell. His revelations were denied her. She had no more visions. She took part in communal devotion, heard the mass, sang in the choir and—conversed in the parlor. She shared the routine of everyday life of all the other nuns, but still—she was not submerged in it.

She was destined to be a saint. And destiny is a power which may take a detour but does not lose sight of its goal and moves through the darkness of night clairvoyantly toward fulfillment.

After Theresa had renounced spiritual prayer for a year and a half, her father died. At his deathbed she met the Dominican friar Vincente de Barrone. To the end he had been Don Alonso's father confessor. The trust which her deceased father had put, during his lifetime, into the experience and wisdom of his spiritual guide, was part of Theresa's heritage. At her father's bier she went up to the monk and disclosed to him the worries of her restive soul. How she had abandoned spiritual prayer, the motives that had induced her to do so, all these things she revealed and held back nothing, not even the faintest sin of thought.

It was the confession of a saint. The Dominican friar saw only a contrite Carmelite nun and failed to find in all her self-accusations the slightest trace of sin. Her visits in the parlor were in keeping with an established convention sanctioned by the "mitigated rule." Her conversations through the grate were a form of distraction which violated none of the pious rules. He reassured Theresa, absolved her from guilt by virtue of the authority vested in him by the church, and encouraged her to resume her spiritual prayer.

This good monk of Ávila, who could not see beyond the horizon of his parish, failed to grasp the conflict in Theresa's soul, and yet his advice was decisive in the further development of her sainthood.

The time which Theresa had spent without spiritual prayer she described later as the most miserable time of her life. When Barrone advised her to resume her silent communion with God, she felt greatly relieved, for during her self-imposed exile on earth she had been constantly harassed by nostalgic thoughts of heaven. Yet the joy of her absolution by the Dominican father confessor was not to remain free from renewed torment. When she did resume her spiritual prayer, her mystic visions appeared again too, but, at the same time and almost automatically, also her former pangs of conscience. Now, when the divine happiness, which she had already given up as lost, came back to her, she became still more painfully aware of the discrepancy between parlor and cell. Vincente de Barrone, to whom the sight of God had never been revealed, could see no harm in her presence in the parlor. But she, whom God had chosen, who had communed with God in immediate contact, felt the crushing weight of the incompatibility of the two worlds. "I suffered much in prayer," she complains, "for the spirit was slave, not master, so that I was unable to withdraw into myself without at the same time enclosing within me a thousand vanities."

In her mental agony she went from one confessor to another. They all listened to her in paternal benevolence, but no one understood her, for what St. Theresa felt to be sinful, the Church had not thought of including in its lists of sins. It lay outside the scope of human laws. Her destiny caused her to be stricter than the rules of the convent, more saintly than the Church, more pious than the most pious of the pious.

Her conscience was more sensitive than that of her confessors. It spoke the language of penitence, which only those can understand who have experienced the grace of creative concentration and know therefore about the sin against the spirit, the sin of distraction and dissipation. Men like St. Bernard, the saint of contemplation, or the mystic Master Eckart would have been able to grasp it; but also men like Newton, who confessed that he could discover the laws of gravity only because he had learned to resist all forms of diverting temptation. Theresa had to follow her road alone, not understood by even the best among the Christians of her century.

For the present, however, her intentions of renouncing the parlor, were not strong enough. Her human will and all its efforts did not suffice. She might have gone on, stumbling and rising, until, as she puts it herself, "she had fallen headlong into hell," if the prayer of quiet and mystic experience had not accomplished what the most pious exertions of will had not been able to do. Her spiritual strength kept growing. It grew in immediacy and vigor and came to play an ever more important part in her life, until it could finally reshape her entire existence, her whole destiny.

One day the clock of the convent was again striking the hour of the parlor. This time it called the nun Theresa even more temptingly than usual out of her cell down into the sphere of worldliness; for one, whom she cared greatly to see again, was waiting there for her. Her love of men was tainted with the weakness which marks all human love. She came to single out one "certain one" among them all and preferred him and liked his conversation best. Now, when the convent clock struck, Theresa left cell and heaven and God and hurried downstairs into the parlor where the preferred one was anxiously waiting for her to appear.

She was up to her ears engaged with him in harmless conversation, so absorbed, so forgetful of everything around her, that it came to her as a shock and took away her breath, when she suddenly perceived right next to the bodily shape of her caller the bodiless figure of Him who often came to see her in the solitude of her cell. "I was greatly astonished and perturbed," she admits. God, in the person of the Savior, had followed her into the parlor. "Christ stood before me," she continues, "stern and grave, giving me to understand what in my conduct was offensive to Him. I saw Him with the eyes of the soul more distinctly than I could have seen Him with the eyes of the body."

The "preferred one," stricken with worldly blindness, kept up his casual chatter. Theresa answered no more. She observed in utter confusion that while her earthly caller talked on and on, her heavenly visitor persisted in silence. One caller looked at her with courting admiration; the other looked at her sternly and with his wordless reproach attracted all her attention. Theresa's eyes and ears were ever more concentrated on the silent apparition and paid no heed to the loquacious guest from town. He, "the preferred one," had been quite confident that this was the day when his irresistible charm would overcome the chastity of pretty Theresa, and now he found himself face to face with a distraught nun who did not look at him but stared into empty space, who did not answer his questions but stood there in deathlike silence, separated from him by the grate of the parlor, deeply absorbed in wordless conversation with the air, with nobody, nothing. He left, sorely disappointed. Theresa did not see him go. And when the visiting hour was over, she was still standing in back of the grate in the parlor; in empty space; rigid and motionless.

The nuns, who knew about her illness, realized that this was again one of the attacks which visited her from time to time. They carried her back to her cell and put her on her cot.

This incident lasted but an hour in the afternoon of a day in 1542, but in timeless time it measured an eternity. Theresa recovered quickly from the attack, and for a while it seemed as though the convent routine would be continued as usual.

From the beginning books had played in Theresa's life the role of guideposts on her pilgrimage to God. A book showed the girl, enmeshed in the pleasures of life, the road to the convent. A book led the nun, trapped in the motions of formal devoutness, onto the road of contemplation. A book revealed to the patient, ridden by pain, the saving road of endurance which Job had pursued. And now it was to be again a book that led her on. By accident she came across the Confessions of St. Augustine, and reading them she thought, as she expressed it later on, that she was seeing her own self. This saint, who had waveringly and heedlessly moved along on his road to God, and who had yet attained his goal, revealed to Theresa the path of her destiny.

This path led past a column in the convent cloister on which a picture was hung of the Savior under the crown of thorns. The prioress had had it erected there in memory of the passion of the Lord, in preparation for the approaching Easter procession. In the ranks of the one hundred and eighty Carmelites of the Incarnation on their way to mass, marched the nun Theresa. When the procession reached the column, the nuns looked in pious emotion at the suffering Son of God and made the sign of the cross. But contrary to plans, they had to stop; for one of the nuns, Teresa de Cepeda, fell out of line, broke down on her knees in front of the image and burst into desperate sobs. The sisters tried to calm her and to lead her back to her place in the procession. But Theresa was in the fullest sense of the word "beside herself." She saw what none of the other nuns could see. In place of the image she saw the Redeemer Himself in all His divinity. A few steps away from her He suffered the martyr's death for the salvation of mankind.

The nun Theresa, kneeling before the Lord, wept over her daily betrayal of Him who had taken upon Himself the suffering of all men. Shame, self-accusation and repentance burst forth in a stream of tears. "The very sight," she writes, "so moved me that my heart was breaking. How ill had I repaid these wounds!"

The other nuns saw in this incident only a morbid fit; and that the procession might go on, the saint was led away.

Almost all, who followed the road to God, had to pass through the "dark gate of penitence." St. Augustine, just like Theresa, burst into violent sobs when he crossed its threshold.

To the mystic, repentance is a second birth into a higher world. As the infant greets the light of this world with weeping, so those, who are reborn in the spirit, greet with tears the light of the heavenly world.

The nun Theresa, reborn in repentance, knelt one morning in the year 1558 together with the other nuns, absorbed in prayer, in the chapel of the Incarnation. The nuns intoned the hymn *Veni Creator*. Together with them Theresa sang: "*Veni Creator*, come Creator Spirit." But in her the voice of repentance was singing. The Creator, who hears everything, heard the song of the nuns. He heard their voices and among them the voice of Theresa. But in Theresa's voice he heard also her penitent prayer. Through eons and eternities he heard her call and answered it and came down into time, down to the earth, to the little chapel of the convent of the Incarnation at Ávila. He freed Theresa's soul from her body, led it away from the chapel, away from time, up to its home in the kingdom of heaven and had it look down from there upon life on earth. How futile it looked! Futile the earth and life in time and space, and doubly futile the parlor of the Incarnation! And as Theresa's soul looked down from such angelic heights on the things of the world, she heard a voice that said: "I will not have you converse with men but with angels!"

Although Theresa's body with all its natural functions and all its organs and senses had remained here below while her soul was raised into heaven, she not only heard these words more distinctly than ever a bodily ear can hear what is said, she also saw and recognized more unmistakably than ever a bodily eye or physical perception are able to do, that it was the Lord Himself who spoke to her.

As long as her soul was bound to her material body, she was subject to human weakness and human ambiguities. But now, when the soul was freed from the body, the bondage of matter and with it material weakness had vanished. The Lord Himself had granted her guidance, as none of his servants on earth, no priest, no father confessor, had been able to do, however much she was in need of it. In that moment of ecstasy Theresa's destiny was fulfilled.

Then her soul returned to its body. Theresa returned to space and time, to the convent chapel in Ávila, to the morning of a day in the year 1558, and all her senses were given back to her. Only one thing the Lord had retained in heaven: her will. But this will in heaven continued to be active in her on earth. "From that day," she wrote, "my resolution to give up everything for His sake became unshakable." She had overcome her worldly leanings. She herself divided her life in two periods, her own life and her life of God, which was to begin now. It began in martyrdom. And the Church, enmeshed in the things of the earth, marked out her Via Dolorosa.

Filled with exuberant joy Theresa hastened to her confessor, Fray Gaspar Daza. She had just seen the Lord of the Church, had seen Him and heard Him, more really and more truly than anything in the world. But the confessor looked at her suspiciously and said sternly: "The devil has deceived your senses." And with all the authority of his office as God's vicar on earth, he admonished Theresa to resist henceforth such "visitations."

The pious nun tried to obey. But God was stronger than Daza's command. The next time she appeared at the confessional she had to admit, quite intimidated and fearful: "He has come again." Amazed and terrified by the obstinacy of the devil, who had chosen to settle down in a nun of his own parish, Daza refused indignantly to lend his pious ear ever again to this victim of hellish wiles.

The venerable priest, Fray Gaspar Daza, was a conscientious officer of the church and liked to keep order in his spiritual affairs. To his way of thinking God's revelations had been settled once and for all by the Church Fathers at their councils, and the church had fulfilled them in its creed and doctrine. That God should suddenly overthrow this neatly ordered tradition and come out with an irregular extra revelation, that He should choose for this purpose a Carmelite nun who often fell victim to morbid attacks, seemed more than doubtful to him. The whole thing looked much rather like a decoy stunt perpetrated by the devil in his endeavor to compromise the faith.

The refusal of the distinguished pastor to receive Theresa at the confessional entailed grave consequences. Most of the sisters and many of her former friends drew away from her. Used to being courted, she was shunned now, and only a very few remained faithful to her. She would doubtless have become involved with the Inquisition, if it had not been for the fact that at this time the militant disciples of Ignatius of Loyola came to Ávila, where they settled down at the monastery of San Gil and took Theresa under their protection.

The Society of Jesus was imbued with an entirely new spirit, and the Jesuit confessors were experts in psychological understanding and guidance. Ignatius, the founder of their order, who at Manresa had at times had visions himself, had taught them that visions are by no means the privilege of chosen saints of past ages, but that God may choose to grant them to anyone, at any time. But Ignatius, who had experienced visions of Christ just like Theresa, had also at times been deceived by devilish tricks, and in order to distinguish truth from deception, he had devised a whole system of controls which he put down in his *Spiritual Exercises*. To those who knew how to apply these exercises correctly, they constituted a most reliable testing device.

The Jesuit fathers approached Theresa without fear or prejudice. That she was a contemporary and just an ailing human being, did not mean for them that God could not possibly have appeared to her in the person of the Redeemer, and whether her visions were of God or the devil would be established by relevant tests.

Padre Diego de Cetinas, Padre Juan de Padranos, one Jesuit father after another had Theresa go through the exercises and devised ever new control experiments. The zeal of the venerable fathers was increased by the benevolent interest which the new general of the order, Francis de Borgia, formerly Duke of Candia, had shown in the visions of the Carmelite nun. For him, who had also been granted many a token of divine grace, one conversation with Theresa was enough to convince him of the truth and divinity of her visions.

The old-established representatives of the church watched meanwhile suspiciously what the Jesuit newcomers were doing. They even induced the prioress of the Incarnation to refuse the Jesuit confessors access to the convent. But then a well-known and wealthy lady, Doña Guiomir de Ulloa, a devoted friend of Theresa's as well as a liberal benefactress of the Incarnation, intervened and obtained permission to take Theresa for a while to her home, where the Jesuits were free to come and go as they pleased.

At this time Padre Baltasar Alvarez took over Theresa's spiritual guidance. His task was to complete the investigations of her unusual case. He was only twenty-four years old and had but recently been ordained. In spite of his youth he was the pride of tin Castilian province of his order, mainly because of his extraordinary learning, his perspicacity and his unrelenting austerity.

Theresa suffered greatly under him, and groaningly she submitted to the mortifications he imposed upon her. This young man was so exacting in his questions and demands, that the feeble middle-aged nun found it hard to keep up with him. "He ordered the affairs of my soul and disquieted me much," she wrote late "Yet it was he, who did me the most good." And then she added with that characteristic humor of hers, "I love this father very much, although he has a bad disposition."

At this time Theresa was overwhelmed by visions. Once the resurrected Christ appeared to her in His sacrosanct humanity in unspeakable beauty and majesty; then again He came invisibly so that not even the inner eye could see Him while yet Theresa knew about his presence with unmistakable assurance. At times she saw the Trinity, then again a host of angels. One vision followed another, and after a while they came no longer sporadically but in coherent succession. Often she lived for days and weeks in a visionary trance. She felt at home in the world beyond as others do here below, and the events over there occurred for her with as much reality as for us the events of the earth.

When she gave Alvarez such heavenly reports, he was carried away and had to remind himself that he must not forget his duties as an examiner. From the beginning he had had faith in the divinity of her visions, but since he was expected to supply proofs, he thought of ever-new ways of putting her to the test.

In order to exclude even the slightest possibility of deception, he extended the exercises to her spiritual life. He took away from her every kind of edifying book, for he wanted to be sure that her visions were not just the product of her imagination which such reading matter might stimulate. During these spiritual fasts Theresa suffered agonies of want and privation. But then, one day, the Lord appeared and said: "Do not grieve", my daughter. I will give you a living book."

To tighten the spiritual discipline still further, Alvarez went so far as to forbid Theresa's spiritual prayers. Then the Lord appeared again and said in an angry tone of voice: "This is certainly tyranny!"

These last two visions influenced Alvarez to such an extent that he decided to conclude his exhaustive investigations. But just at that moment the scandal broke loose in Ávila. Theresa's visions had become the talk of the town, and the whole place was divided into two camps. The ones saw in Theresa a saint, the others—and they were the majority—an impostor who deceived her confessor and should be tried by the Inquisition. Her adversaries went so far as to compare her to Magdalena de la Cruz, that notorious "visionary of Cordoba," by whom even the Grand Inquisitor and the queen had been duped and who finally, unmasked as a swindler, had stood before her judges in wretched misery with a rope around her neck and a candle in her hands.

When Theresa came again to the confessional, speaking of a vision in which the Lord had appeared to her in a formless form, Alvarez looked at her distrustfully. In a formless form? The gossip about town, the warning case of Magdalena de la Cruz, the threatening shadow of the Inquisition, all these things made him stop, and more severely than ever he took Theresa to task.

"How do you know that it was He, since you did not see Him?" he asked curtly.

"I do not know how. All I can say with certainty is the fact that I did see the Lord near me."

"But how did He reveal Himself?"

"It was no sensory vision and I saw no form. I saw nothing with the eyes of my body. I saw nothing with the eyes of my soul. But I felt His presence at my side."

"If you saw Him neither with your eyes of the body nor with your eyes of the soul, how then can you maintain that it was He?

Who told you?"

"He Himself did," she said. "But even before He let me know, it was impressed upon my soul with much greater assurance than perception by the senses could have supplied."

"How did you hear His words?" Alvarez asked.

"I heard no words. It was some other means by which the Lord conveyed His thoughts to me. But it was all much clearer to me than a spoken word could ever have been. I understood very deep mysteries about the truth which is Truth Itself. It has neither beginning nor end. O my Lord, what difference there is between hearing these words and comprehending their significance in such a way! I comprehended it all although my words are obscure compared with so much clarity."

Alvarez was utterly confused. He was ready to believe Theresa, but her story was hard to grasp, even for one whose reason was rooted in faith.

The venerable representatives of the church with Daza at their head came to Alvarez and insisted, "She is deceiving you! She is deceiving you!"

He called Theresa and asked her, "Do you really believe the things you have told me or have you told them only to deceive me?"

She replied: "I have said nothing but the truth."

Before letting her go, Alvarez warned her again: "Think twice!

Is it really as you have told me or have you allowed yourself to be deceived by chimerical fancies? Probe yourself! You owe it to our holy faith."

Obediently Theresa searched her soul. But after a while the formless form appeared to her in a vision and spoke: "Be not troubled, my daughter, it is I."

She went and confessed: "The Lord has confirmed it."

Alvarez buried himself in learned books and writings. He read every authoritative account of visions he could find. He read for days and nights and the books kept piling up on his desk. Once a fellow Jesuit asked him why he had to work through all this material and he replied angrily: "I must read all these books, because I want to understand the Carmelite nun Theresa." Finally his efforts were rewarded. In the *Summa Theologiae* of St. Thomas Aquinas he came across a passage presenting in extremely learned terms an account of visions which are not perceived through the senses but in species impressa, by immediate conception through the intellect. He learned that in such intellectual visions and locutions the revelation of the Lord is given, without sensory mediation, into the power of understanding. The Doctor Angelicus called this type of vision even more reliable than any other because the exclusion of the senses excluded also every kind of self-deception. So there were divine visions of the kind Theresa said she had had! His reliance on her truthfulness was justified.

But the pack of doubters did not relent. Now they even insisted that Theresa should be exorcised. Alvarez, however, would not be intimidated. Encouraged by his newly acquired knowledge he set himself up as Theresa's defender. But whether it was merely a coincident or whether the devil had really a hand in it, just when Alvarez was ready to come out in public with his pleadings on behalf of Theresa, he was sent away on a tour of inspection and a locum tenens took his place.

Now the long-awaited moment for Daza and his group had come. It could not be difficult to intimidate the deputy confessor. On the strength of their rank in the hierarchy of the church they came to him with the demand that he should exorcise the obsessed nun and cast out her devilish hallucinations. Yielding to their pressure the deputy confessor had recourse to a most brutal means. He ordered Theresa to ward off the next apparition by a disdainful and spurning gesture. "Give it the fig!" he said. "If it is the devil, he may take it as an expression of your contempt, and if it is the Lord, He will not hold it against you, for you are merely obeying an order which I have given you to protect our holy faith."

With great qualms Theresa obeyed. "This business of giving the fig," she relates, "caused me the greatest sorrow, for my next vision was one of the suffering Lord. When I saw Him present before one, I could not believe, if they cut me to pieces, that it was the devil, and so it was a heavy penance for me. I begged Him to pardon me, since I did it to obey the one He had put in His place. He [374] told me not to worry about it, since He would make the Truth understood."

When Alvarez returned to Ávila, the whole town was in a ferment over Theresa's visions. Her last remaining friends, with the exception of Doña Guiomir, had deserted her. And the scandal had gone beyond the walls of Ávila. All of Spain was discussing Theresa's visions, and in its excitement the public demanded ever more insistently that the case of the Carmelite visionary be investigated by the Inquisition.

Only a few steps away from San Gil, which was now occupied by the Jesuits, stood the Dominican monastery of San Tomas, where the body of the Grand Inquisitor Torquemada lay entombed. The spirit of this man, who had died but a generation ago, was still terrifyingly alive. The machinery of the Inquisition continued to function with swiftness and precision. Everywhere in Spain the pyres were blazing on which heretics and witches were purged by death in the flames.

Those who wanted to see Theresa delivered into the hands of the Inquisition, began to mention the name of Alvarez in connection with hers. Then even he, her last spiritual support, became uncertain, and she feared, as she puts it, that she would have no one to hear her confession, but that everyone would flee from her. "I did nothing but weep," she adds. Yet in the midst of this general turmoil the Lord appeared to her and said: "Be not afraid, my daughter, I shall not abandon you."

Theresa knew with absolute certainty that it was the Lord who appeared to her, yet—all the world suspected her. She spoke nothing but the truth, yet—they called her a liar. She saw the Redeemer face to face, Him for whom the bells tolled, for whom the masses were celebrated, whom all of Christendom beseeched in pious prayer, yet—the reverend priests of the church persecuted her, called Him, who appeared to her, the devil, and wanted to drag her before the judges of the Inquisition. Her father confessor heard the confession of her soul, but he did not trust her. How could he fail to understand that the words she transmitted to him had been given her by the One who had ordained him? She had seen the Savior and brought His message to the Christian world but the Christian world did not want to listen.

Her human mind could never have grasped all this; it would have had to break down. Her human heart could never have borne all the undeserved pain; it would have had to despair. But Theresa was one of the elect. Her decisions were made in heaven; her knowledge came to her by revelation; her strength was won in ecstasy; her grief was shared by the Lord.

When heaven came down to earth in her visions, when the Lord spoke to her in His revelation, the deep significance of all her suffering became apparent. It was transfigured into heavenly bliss. One day, when she could hardly bear it any longer, it came to pass, while she was kneeling in prayer in Doña Guiomir home, that an angel appeared to her at her side. "I saw him," she writes, "close by in bodily form, on my left hand. He was short of stature but exceedingly beautiful. By his burning countenance I knew him for one of those spirits of the highest rank, who seem to be wholly fire: they must be those whom we call Cherubim. I saw in his hand a long dart of gold, and at the end of the iron there seemed to be a little fire. This, I thought, he thrust through my heart several times so that it reached my very entrails. So real was the pain that I was forced to moan aloud, yet it was so surpassingly sweet that I could not wish to be delivered from it. No delight of life can give more content. As the angel withdrew the dart, he left me all burning with a great love of God. So dazed was I with this pain and glory together, that I could not understand how it could be. Yet it is such a delightful language of love that passed then between my soul and God that I beg of His goodness that He may give the enjoyment of it to him who may think I lie."

She did not dare to speak about it to Alvarez, for the splendor of it was too dear to her heart to expose it to doubt and distrust. For days she was totally absorbed by this experience, she spoke to no one and avoided all contact with men. But the pent-up bliss demanded expression and found it in one of her most tenderly fervent poems:

In the very depth of my being
I have been stricken and, oh,
The hand was surely Divine,
Such marvels followed the blow.

Though the dart has wounded me sore,

35

visibly true.

History relates that one day—it was a holiday and many had come to attend mass—Theresa was kneeling before the altar, when she was suddenly carried away in ecstatic raptures. Before the eyes of all present, the kneeling nun hovered above the ground. Her face, the story adds, was transfigured in such supernatural beauty that all were seized in awe and veneration.

At this time the Inquisition was still the domain of the Dominicans. Pedro de Ibañez, the prior of St. Thomas, who was well-acquainted with the proceedings of the Inquisition, advised Theresa to forestall action against her by putting her case up to the Inquisition herself, submitting a written account of her life and her visions. Thus the first version of Theresa's famous *Vida* came to be written.

Ibañez' advice was good. The examiners of the Inquisition studied the deposition of the Carmelite nun with conscientious distrust, scrutinizing it for the most hidden trace of heresy or deceit. But all their prejudiced pedantry could not detect enough evidence to justify proceedings against her. To be entirely on the safe side, they submitted the document for inspection to the Dominican Banes, who was feared for his inexorable strictness. He read it with a trained eye and recognized in it proof of divine revelation. Instead of the expected verdict of guilty, the Holy Office issued a brief of recommendation, in which it was stated that the reading of Theresa's *Vida* would serve to strengthen the faith and to edify the faithful.

The town of Ávila, the Christian church and the world at large might have decided to tolerate and accept the visionary nun. Theresa might have settled down to live in the quiet of her cell, unmolested and fully absorbed by her divine visions. But just as the girl Theresa, upon entering the convent, had not been destined to live the normal life of an average nun, so the visionary Carmelite, in the grace of God, was not destined to lead a life fully contained in mystic contemplation. It was her mission to know the heavens, be at home among angels, and, at the same time, live on earth and act among men. The last twenty years of her life show us a practical and active woman, untiringly engaged in the reform of her order, and founding, within this period of time, seventeen new convents. Her practical work in the world and her contemplative life, however, must not be taken as two unrelated sides of her nature. In her all was one and of a piece. As her illness and her visions sprang from the same source, so her contemplation and her active life had one and the same origin. Her labors in the world endeavored to build the house of silence and were thus concerned with leading the order of the Carmelites back to the road of its original destination.

To provide silence with a home on earth, the first Carmelite house had been erected on lonely Mount Carmel. When the Carmelite hermits migrated west, they brought with them on their lips and in their hearts the silence of Lebanon, and their first monasteries in Europe were built after the model of Eastern retreats from the world. Since then centuries had gone by, and the homes of contemplation of the old Carmelites had become centers of social life for nuns and monks.

Theresa's plan for monastic reforms had its roots in direct personal experience. She had spent three years outside the walls of the convent. In the home of her pious friend Doña Guiomir she had enjoyed the privilege of perfect seclusion, which made it possible for her to be ready, any hour, day or night, for meditation, vision or devotional exercise. During this time she lived in an almost uninterrupted mystical union with God. Now her leave had come to an end, and she returned from the world to her convent. A group of noisy nuns received her. She withdrew to her cell to contemplate God. But the convent bell rang. The hour of the parlor had come. Theresa wanted to remain in her cell. But the nuns came to call for her. In the parlor visitors were waiting. In front of her, set off by the token bars of a flimsy grate, was the bustle of worldly life, were gossip and trinkets, flattery and gifts. She felt she was roasted on the grates of worldliness. She tried to escape, but in vain. The world was part of the daily routine of the convent. Again and again contemplation was interrupted by idle diversions, humility was misled by vanity, poverty by gifts.

As long as she herself had been a victim of these temptations, her desperate struggles had been merely concerned with her own salvation. She had been weak and had seen nothing beyond her own weakness. She had been guilty and had not looked beyond her guilt. But now she had overcome the dangers of worldliness in her own soul and recognized the greater guilt beyond her individual guilt, the guilt of the secularized convent, of the mitigated rule of the Carmelite order, which tried to please God and the world at the same time.

"Oh what utter ruin!" she exclaimed. "What utter ruin of religious persons, where the same monastery offers two roads, one of virtue and observance, the other of unobservance, and both equally frequented. The poor things are not at fault, for they walk in the way that is shown them. Many of them are to be pitied."

But were the "poor things" of the Incarnation the only ones to be pitied? In all the Carmelite convents and monasteries of the mitigated rule, the souls of nuns and monks were confused by the two roads. Theresa herself had risen above the dangers of such temptation. But she was not one of those who are smugly satisfied with the salvation of their own souls. To have been saved implied for her the duty of trying to save others. God had given Himself to her in secret, so that she might give herself openly to others. On silence was built the house of the Lord, which she had been made to see in her ecstasies, so that she might build it again on earth to help her sisters. In silence she had found the way of redemption; she had been led to find it so that she might be able to show it to others.

If her plan had sprung exclusively from practical considerations, she would have had to abandon it at the very first thought. Here she was, a nun, who had nothing to her name but the clothes she was wearing, and decided to found a convent, quite aware of the fact that it was a venture which called for considerable financial backing. A visionary, at home in another world, took up the struggle with hard realities, with cunning men, with jealous nuns, intriguing churchmen, with all the caprices, the thoughtlessness and inconstancy of the world. An ailing creature, who had spent the greater part of her life on the sickbed, who had now reached the age of fifty-seven, took on a burden of work, the strain of which might well have taxed the strength of a youthful person in the pink of health. A woman of sixteenth-century Spain, living at an age and in a country whose traditions and conventions excluded women from participation in all public activities,

Though the wound be even to death,
With a pain beyond any on earth,
Yet this wound alone gives me breath!

It kills,—how then does it give life?
It gives life,—how can it destroy?
How, while wounding, still heal, leaving thee
Closest union with God to enjoy?

Divine skill must belong to the Hand,
Whose lance in a combat so dire,
Passes through, yet gives life to the foe,
Whom it bends to the Victor's desire.

Meanwhile Theresa's concerns on earth had not taken a turn for the better. All the world was against her, but the grace of Heaven was with her. Just when the turmoil at Ávila had reached its peak and all were clamoring with one voice, "Take her to the Inquistion! To the Inquisition!" the vociferating voices were suddenly silenced by an unexpected event. Fray Pedro de Alcántara, the town crier of the Lord, had come to Ávila, and everybody was streaming to the market place where the emaciated ascetic, bare footed, a living skeleton clothed in sackcloth, was addressing the crowd. Alcántara was famous throughout Spain, for it was said that in him St. Francis had come back to life. Just like St. Francis he walked through the woods and praised in joyful songs the glories of God's creation. And so deeply was he imbued with the spirit of St. Francis that he had set himself the task of reforming the failing Franciscan order. He had founded several monasteries in which the Franciscan monks were living again as humble servants of their Lady Poverty.

The crowds claimed the attention of the holy man all for themselves, but it seemed that he had come to Ávila only to see the one: Teresa de Cepeda. When he came face to face with her for the first time, it was as though they had known one another all along. They welcomed each other as citizens of the City of God and conversed with each other in the native tongue of heaven.

Theresa had found her knight. Alcántara shielded her against all attacks and defended her truthfulness. His first victory was triumph won over the doubts in the mind of Father Alvarez, and with him many friends, who had fallen away, came back to Theresa. But Alcántara made also new friends for her, among them Fray Pedro de Ibañez, the prior of the Dominican monastery of San Tomas, and Gaspar De Salazar, the rector of San Gil, the new home of the Jesuits. Finally Alcántara's protestations succeeded even in convincing Theresa's archenemy, the distrustful Daza, of the divinity of her visions.

When many of her adversaries persisted in their campaign of calumnies, the moment had come for God to fulfill His promise. "I shall make the truth understood!" had been the wordless words of the invisible vision, and now it was to become audibly and chose a task, which would bring her into the limelight of public attention. The child of an era, which had given itself up to worldliness, undertook a work, which ran counter to the most powerful trend of the times. A nun of the Carmelite order of the mitigated rule was bold enough to break with monastic forms which, since their initiation through Pope Eusebius a century ago, had established themselves as consecrated customs. And all this she did without breaking her vow of absolute obedience.

In the end her passionate wish to succeed won out against all odds. The capital needed was suddenly at hand, unsolicited and as a matter of course, as though it had just been waiting for a chance to be of service to her. Her ailing body proved equal to all hardships, as though the strain of a busy life and the infirmities of age could not harm it, because it had been steeled by the "little deaths" through which it had passed. Untiringly she traveled in her spring-less cart, on wretched roads, in all directions through the Spanish countryside. She bartered and bargained, complained and protested, arranged and organized, and in the midst of all hazards, the aging woman preserved the smiling courage, the cheerful heart of a girl who takes delight in the prospect of adventure, the challenge of adversities.

She who felt at home in heaven proved to know her way about on earth: The visionary, fighting for her foundation, developed amazing skill in dealing with business men and traders, and none of the intricacies of bills of sale and financial calculations could ever be too much for her. In her negotiations she was an astute diplomat and mastered the art of making friends of adversaries, helpers of persecutors. She had a way of reducing pride to humility, of catching the shrewd in their own stratagems, of turning accusations against the accuser. The keenness of her mind caused a dignitary of the church, who had entered upon a theological discussion with her, to exclaim in despair: "Great God, I would rather argue with all the theologians in the world than with this woman!" And a priest, to whom she had come with a letter of introduction, wrote after her visit to his correspondent: "You spoke in your letter of a nun, but you have sent me a bearded man!"

The genius of this holy woman overcame all difficulties, all the confusion and all the treachery of the world. In the end, Spain, the country where women were considered incapable of greatness, prided itself with having given to the world, in the person of Theresa, one of the greatest women of all times; and the church, which had opposed her aspirations, canceled for her sake a papal decree, abandoned old-established customs, and received her, primarily on account of her reform of the Carmelite order, into the community of the saints.

Theresa's career as a reformer, which progressed through risks, adventures and dramatic complications, began as a peaceful convent idyll. In the course of a casual conversation, her long dreamed-of ideal appeared suddenly within range of possible realization. After a holiday mass, which had been read in the chapel of the Incarnation, Theresa returned to her cell with a few fellow nuns and a niece of hers, María de Ocampo, who had come for a visit, and spoke to them about the celebration they had just witnessed. The concert-hall style of music and all the pomp and display, she felt, were made to appeal to worldly guests rather than to God and the mass as a whole was much more of a public performance than a devotional exercise. The folly of it all deepened her longing for a home of quiet and devotion, undisturbed by the worldly bustle of intruding guests, a home of the kind the founders of her order had had on Mt. Carmel. Now she discussed these things with her friends. But what she said was formulated only as the vague wish of a devout nun. Then Theresa's niece interrupted her in her reveries with the question why such a home could not be established. "Mainly," Theresa replied, "because we have not the means." But that María could not accept as a valid excuse, and with the quick and ready enthusiasm of youth she offered her heritage as the initial capital for the foundation.

The moment the dream struck root in earthly realities, the dreamer proved that she could stand firmly with both feet on solid ground. To carry out her plan she needed, in addition to the initial capital, the consent of the provincial of the order. She lacked all worldly experience, but suddenly she knew her way about in the affairs of the world. Protection smoothes the way to success. And so she started out by seeking, in pursuit of a well-thought-out plan, the endorsement of three men whom she knew to be favorably inclined toward her and who, respectively, were representatives of three of the most influential monastic orders: St. Alcántara, the Franciscan; St. Francisco de Borgia, the general of the Jesuits; and Fray Luis de Bertran, the famous Dominican. When letters of recommendation from these men had arrived, she asked Doña Guiomir to take them to the provincial of the Carmelites and to ask him for his dispensation. In Doña Guiomir Theresa had made an excellent choice. She was a generally respected widow, who liked to have a hand in the mediation of holy affairs, and had made a name for herself as a liberal benefactress of the Carmelite order. The provincial, Angel de Salazar, facing this noble lady and seeing the letters of recommendation spread out before him, could not very well withhold his consent, for the petition was a pious one and the funds were at hand.

Now Theresa could begin to look for a house. She found what seemed to her well suited for the purpose she had in mind and proceeded to draw up the bill of sale. Only the signatures remained to be affixed. Then the storm at the Incarnation broke loose. "What dreadful treachery!" exclaimed the prioress when she heard of Theresa's plans for a rival foundation. "That arrogant little fool!" the nuns chimed in. "This convent of ours is not good enough for her, she thinks."

Soon the excitement of the convent affected all of Ávila. Amongst the townspeople the nuns found ready allies in their wrath. "A nun trying to draw up bills of sale! Let her stay in the convent where she belongs," jeered the men. And the women added: "As for that patroness of hers, that Doña Guiomir, she had better take care of her orphaned children!" The whole town was in a rage.

When the prioress went to remonstrate with the provincial, her protests were supported by a delegation of vociferating burghers. Under the pressure of public opinion Salazar withdrew his consent, using a technicality as a pretext. He had overlooked, he said, that the available funds were not at all sufficient to support the new convent after it had been founded.

Theresa was disappointed but not discouraged. The provincial had not the last word in the matter. Above him, at the head of the entire hierarchy of the Church, was the Holy Father in Rome, and a papal dispensation would overrule any decision of a provincial. This nun, who looked out at the world from the secluded safety of her cell, was amazingly shrewd in her understanding of practical matters and knew immediately of a way of bringing her problem to the attention of Rome. She enlisted the help of Fray Pedro de Ibañez, the prior of the Dominican monastery of St. Thomas. Ibañez had not deserted her when all of Ávila had suspected her visions. Ibañez would help her now to realize her plans for a home of truly Christian devotion. The Dominican order was the most reliable support of Roman power in Spain. And then there was the personal reputation which Ibañez, one of the most eminent Thomists of his time, enjoyed at the Papal See. A suggestion from him was sure to be favorably received by the Holy Father.

The Carmelite provincial sensed new complications when he heard about the frequent visits which the Dominican prior paid to Theresa, the black sheep among his nuns. He could not object openly to the interest which so high-ranking a churchman took in Theresa's ideas, but he ought to be able to think of a move, which would quietly eliminate the Dominican's unwelcome interference. He was an absolute master within his domain; and if he chose to do so, he could simply remove the embarrassing nun from the scene. It did not take him long to find a satisfactory pretext.

In Toledo the Duke de la Cerda had just died. His wife Luise, of the ducal house of Medina Celli, was so overwhelmed with grief that no one in her environment could console her. Her relatives were looking throughout the land for a person able to revive and comfort her. Suddenly it seemed to the provincial that the unbearable grief of the noble and wealthy lady could no longer be tolerated by the Christian world. To relieve her sorrow was the most urgent need of the hour. Now it was a remarkable coincidence that the convent of the Incarnation, which stood under his rule, had a nun whom God visited in her visions and whom many considered a saint. This was surely the person best suited as a companion for the noble lady, who was fastidious in her tastes and would not have thought of receiving an ordinary nun. Luise de la Cerda and all her ducal relatives deigned to be most graciously enthusiastic about the generous offer of the Carmelite provincial and were impatiently waiting for the arrival of the visionary. It was in the middle of winter, shortly before Christmas; the roads were impassable and covered with snow and ice. But the duchess was impatient and the provincial could not wish to prolong the sorrow of so great a lady. Theresa had to leave immediately for Toledo.

Her whole heart was in her projected foundation, whose prospects of realization had grown brighter again through Ibañez' support. All her thoughts were concerned with the question of how she could build her own convent in accordance with the rules of silence and evangelical poverty. But here she went jogging along in her squeaky little cart, on dangerously ice-bound roads, through howling storms, over desolate passes, across the frozen Adaja, was impeded by mountains of snow, and finally, after four days of terrible hardships, arrived in Toledo at the residence of the duchess.

Well-groomed footmen helped her out of her wretched little cart and vied with each other for the privilege of carrying her miserable little box, which contained all her possessions, up into the ducal mansion. Theresa herself was escorted inside with due ceremonies and was taken to the room where the duchess, exhausted by grief, received her in bed. There she lay, surrounded by her deeply concerned relatives who watched anxiously every twitch in her face, every sigh from her lips.

After these introductory ceremonies Theresa was taken to a suite of rooms which was to be henceforth her apartment. In her heart the ideal of a modest convent cell with bare walls, she found herself condemned to live amidst the luxuries of a ducal palace. Imbued with the spirit of Christian humility and the desire to serve, she saw herself persecuted by servile lackeys whose sole duty it was to wait for her orders. She, who required merely a hard crust of bread, had to take part in festive banquets and eat at tables which bent under the burden of food and drink.

The duchess treated her with condescending charm. She read every wish from her eyes and fulfilled even her weird desire for frugal meals and a certain amount of solitude. She allowed her to live in one little room and excused her from all excessive etiquette. Yet Theresa felt like a prisoner in the midst of all this lavish pomp. With her characteristic keenness of observation she summarized her impressions in these terms: "I saw," she said, "how little the power of nobility ought to be esteemed, and how, the greater it is, the more cares and troubles they have;—care to keep the etiquette suitable to their estate, which does not allow them to live or to eat without a fixed time or plan, for everything has to go according to their position and not to their constitutions; many times they have to eat food suitable to their position but not to their taste . .. This is a subjection, and one of the lies the world tells is to call such persons lords and ladies, for to me they seem only slaves of a thousand things."

Theresa rejoiced like a freed woman, when her six months of comforting service were over and when, released from the palace, she traveled again in her springless, squeaky little cart over the roads of Spain, which were now covered with dust and scorched by the sun. For these roads were taking her back to Ávila.

Six months seemed to have been lost, but the stratagem of the provincial had not succeeded in weaning her from her plan. On the contrary, her sojourn in the Toledo palace had only increased her determination. The experience of grotesque riches had demonstrated to her only the more poignantly that the true life in God is possible only in frugal poverty and humble devotion. This excursion into wealth had taught her to appreciate the true freedom which voluntary poverty can bestow. What she has to say on this score shows her deep insight and great wisdom. "Poverty," she writes, "is a strong wall. It is a wealth which includes all the wealth of the world; it is complete possession and dominion. What are kings and lords to me if I do not envy them their riches? True poverty, undertaken for the sake of God, bears with it a certain dignity, in that he who professes it, need seek to please no one but Him; and there is no doubt that the man who asks no help has many friends. If poverty is real, it guards purity and all the other virtues better than fine buildings."

Theresa's return to Ávila coincided with the arrival of a letter from Rome. It brought the reply of the Holy Father and was a papal bull in which Pius IV gave his permission for Theresa's convent.

Theresa's joy was premature. Cardinal de San Angelo, who had drafted the dispensation in the name of the pope, had inadvertently failed to specify under what jurisdiction the new convent should be placed within the organization of the church.

Thus the papal dispensation remained legally invalid until a definite decision could be obtained from Rome as to whether the foundation was to be placed under the protection of the Carmelite order or of the bishop of Ávila.

During the interval Theresa was not idle. Without leaving her cell, she proceeded with the energy of a "bearded man" to make all the necessary arrangements, so that, when the reply from Rome arrived, the consecration of her convent would suffer no further delay. She had learned her lesson from the furor she had caused among the good burghers of Ávila when she, a woman and nun, had dared to buy a house. This time she conducted the negotiations through the agency of her brother-in-law Juan de Ovalle. He had a home in the country, he was entirely unknown in Ávila, and if he bought a house and managed it for Theresa until she was ready to have it consecrated as her convent, he could easily do so, without arousing suspicion, under the pretext that he and his family wanted to move to the city.

But in spite of Theresa's circumspection there remained a good many difficulties that had to be overcome. The house which Juan had bought proved to be in need of alterations. The funds supplied by Theresa's niece had been used up in the purchase, and nobody wanted to bring upon himself the wrath of the entire town by lending his financial support to Theresa's venture. The papal bull arrived with the requested specification and designated the bishop of Ávila as the protector of the new foundation. But the bishop, fearful of the reaction of his town, shifted for subterfuges. Ibañez, who tried to obtain from him a definite commitment, got nowhere, and when Alcántara, from his deathbed, asked for an audience, the bishop fell conveniently ill and withdrew for a rest to his country estate of El Tiemblo.

It began to look as though everybody and everything were conspiring against Theresa's plan, when suddenly things took a turn for the better. A cargo of gold arrived in Seville, and the ship that carried it brought also a small amount of gold for Theresa from her brother Lorenzo in Peru. It was just enough to finance the necessary alterations. Juan de Ovalle's wife had to go to Alba for urgent family reasons. After she had gone, Juan fell seriously ill, and Theresa, who had to nurse him, was given permission to stay away from the convent. Thus she was in a position to direct and supervise the alteration of her house without attracting notice.

Alcántara, on the verge of death, gathered together his remaining strength, climbed on his mule and followed the bishop, who had run away from him, to his retreat in the country. One morning, when the bishop looked out of his window, he saw to his great dismay a skeleton wrapped in sackcloth approaching on the back of a mule. It was Alcántara. This man, who was imbued with the spirit of reform, who himself had initiated the reform of the Franciscan order, regarded the reintroduction of the primitive rule of the Carmelites as an undertaking the support of which was important enough to be the last great task of his life.

His glowing enthusiasm, coupled with the established reputation of his powerful personality, induced the bishop to promise finally that he would forthwith return to Ávila and discuss the matter there with Theresa. After his first conversation with her, the bishop tried no longer to resist the persuasive power of her argument and agreed to place the new convent under his protection.

The consent of the bishop put merely the stamp of official sanction on a plan of reform, worked out by Theresa to the last detail and conceived by her to give to the world the example of a truly God-fearing community. With remarkable circumspection she had thought of all contingencies and worked out a system of defense in depth, which no worldly temptation could pierce. Her institution was to be built on the basis of uncompromising poverty, at a time when all the other monasteries and convents lived on grants and gifts from noble patrons so that they could never be entirely free from a certain dependence on wealth and worldly power. Theresa's new convent was to be supported without grants. Even the begging of alms, practiced by so many religious orders, was banned by Theresa's rules. For begging, too, makes the pious dependent upon the world; and dependence will always generate a spirit of compromise if not of downright obsequiousness. This woman, who had partaken of .the highest bliss through a gift of grace, had come to the conclusion that also the lowlier necessities of life, the daily provisions for her followers and herself, should be left to the grace of Him who provides for the lilies of the field. To make possible the highest form of devotion to God and life eternal, the new convent was to have no parlor but only cells, a chapel and a refectory. The singing nuns were to have no audience but God, and the mass, devoid of pomp and display, was to be celebrated exclusively as a devotional observance. These stringent and simple rules were devised by a woman who knew by experience about the dangers to which the lives of the pious are exposed. They were intended for the new convent, but they were conceived as an example for all Christian devotion. Their main purpose was the reform of the Carmelite order, which at the time of its inception had been a demonstration of such truly Christian devotion.

To recall the original example to the minds of the faithful, Theresa reintroduced also the austere habit of the original Carmelites. Dressed in coarse sackcloth and always barefoot, thus her nuns were to serve their Lord. A minor change in habit, a little reduction of the importance of material things, but the deeper significance of it was the implied rejection of materiality in all things and all respects.

At first the Carmelites had gone barefoot; then they had put on shoes; then Theresa's reform made them barefoot again. The story of the entire order is contained in these stages. Humility was signified by the bare feet which touched the earth of Lebanon. But those who walked west from Mount Carmel put on shoes when they crossed the threshold of modern times, and in doing so they became children of modernity. For not only their feet were hemmed in by the shoes of the time but also their souls, their devotion, their prayers, their piety. On their pilgrimage to God they wore the shoes of worldliness.

The shoe was a symbol of everything else. Barefoot the Carmelites had practiced silence. When they wore shoes they conversed with the world. Barefoot they lived their lives in fervent devoutness. When they wore shoes they looked for relief, for exemptions and relaxation. The frugal fare, the continued fasts of the barefoot Carmelites of early times could not satisfy the members of the order at a later period, when they wore shoes and seasoned their meals and made them attractive with all sorts of dainties and delicacies. Theresa wanted her order to discard shoes, but with them the spirit of worldliness which they represented, and so she called her order the order of the unshod or Discalced Carmelites.

As patron saint of her convent Theresa chose St. Joseph, the father of the Holy Family. It had been St. Joseph whom she had implored more often than any other saint to help her in the trials of her illness, and since he had been merciful, she now placed her convent under his protection.

The purpose of the alterations in Juan de Ovalle's "town house" had been kept a secret, and the final consecration of the building as the convent of St. Joseph was similarly managed without attracting public notice. On St. Bartholomew's Day in the year 1562 the barefoot founder, dressed in sackcloth, knelt absorbed in prayer before the altar, surrounded by her first four nuns. Daza, the same church official who had regarded Theresa as obsessed by the devil, had been delegated by the bishop to consecrate in his name this convent of a saint who wanted to restore the true faith. The four nuns took their vows. They sang the Te Deum. There were no colorful ceremonies, no pomp and no display. But the enraptured nun, who knelt there surrounded by her four disciples at the altar of the little chapel, was kneeling in heaven. And proximity to heaven was to remain the essence of daily life at St. Joseph's.

The nuns of the parlor at the Incarnation felt tricked by the saint and were in a rage. There was nothing they could do against the foundation of the new convent which stood under the protection of the bishop. But the foundress herself was a Carmelite nun who had taken the vow of obedience and was subject to the jurisdiction of her order. It did not come as a surprise, therefore, when the barefoot nun in sackcloth was ordered by her prioress to put on the shoes of worldliness and the white robe of the mitigated rule to appear at the Incarnation and to account for her deeds.

When Theresa entered the refectory she found herself face to face with one hundred and eighty nuns, a court of one hundred and eighty prosecutors, ready to pass judgment against her. The prioress spoke in their name and accused Theresa on the counts of disobedience, arrogance and treachery.—When the time came for determining the form of punishment to be imposed upon her, the jury found itself in an embarrassing position. More rigorous fasts would hardly be a penalty for one who had a veritable mania for fasting; confinement to a solitary cell was precisely what she longed for; exclusion from all social life meant happiness to her; hard work was a blessing and even castigation a welcome humiliation. The culprit deprived all current forms of punishment of their force, for she turned them into rewards, and the only way out was to sentence her to wearing the shoes and the white robe of the mitigated rule and to eating in the refectory and appearing in the parlor; to keep her chained to the easy and comfortable life of the convent, until the men of Avila would find a way of closing the new foundation in spite of papal sanction and of episcopal protection.

The men of Avila stood united behind the nuns of the Incarnation. Rivalries of long standing were forgotten. The contending parties buried the hatchet and took up arms in the common cause. This renitent nun, who had had the impudence of opening a reformed convent in spite of the explicit disapproval voiced by local authorities, who had even succeeded in taking the bishop in, had to be dealt with exemplarily.

A first attempt to rid the town quickly and smoothly of the vexatious convent was undertaken by the prefect of the police. He sent four of his most reliable men to take care of the four nuns at St. Joseph's. But this action wound up in a pitiful failure. Those tough fellows knew how to handle thieves and rowdies and drunkards; they knew how to get access to the most dangerous hide-outs of criminals; but all their experience did them no earthly good, when they had forced their way into the convent and found themselves face to face with four meek and humble virgins of Christ who kept repeating, "God wants us to stay, and so we shall stay!" So much calm determination was more than disconcerting to the worthy guardians of peace and order. They departed without ceremony and swore never to return.

But this fiasco of the police served only to increase the wrath of the town and induced the municipal authorities to throw in their full might against the barefoot nuns. The governor convoked the junta for a solemn session of protest and invited representatives of all the monastic orders whose attitude was deemed to be safe. A unanimous resolution of the governing body was to bring about the closing down of St. Joseph's.

When the bishop of Avila saw that his entire flock went over to the opposition, he fell ill again and left for another rest in the country. Ibañez was away on a tour of inspection, and the prioress of the Incarnation felt obliged to detain Theresa at the convent because of "domestic matters of great urgency" so that it became impossible for her to appear in person and account for her actions before the junta. There seemed to be no obstacle in the way of a quick and smooth resolution.

The occasion was an important one, and the junta convened in great state. The session was noisy, but it was not the noise of clashing viewpoints; it was the noise of a unanimous fury. The governor himself formulated the charge of sedition, danger to the state and disregard for the budgetary interests of the town. None of the representatives of municipal and monastic organizations, who spoke after the governor had finished, saw fit to ask for proof or substantiation. It was all very clear. The convent had to be closed. Everybody agreed with the governor. There was a storm of applause.

Then the representative of the Dominican monastery of St. Thomas, the influential Fray Domingo Banes, got up and spoke. This was unexpected. His words, like a hailstorm from a cloudless sky, came hammering down with sarcastic precision upon the young crop of hate, in which the whole town seemed to take so much pride. "What is it," he inquired ironically, "that has brought us together here? What hostile army has broken into our city? What conflagration endangers Ávila? What kind of pestilence mows down the population? What famine kills thousands of people? What curse threatens our homes? Or are merely four barefoot virgins the cause of all this excitement? I cannot help feeling that the prestige of our city must suffer when so distinguished an assembly must be convoked on account of so insignificant a cause."

The speech was short but it spoiled the artful scheme of the junta. Instead of reaching a decision it had to adjourn in embarrassed confusion. And then it adjourned again and again and again, until the whole matter could quietly be dropped from the agenda.

The bishop returned smiling and in good health. The four nuns at St. Joseph's walked barefoot and prayed and fasted. But the angered provincial of the Carmelites was adamant in his decision that Theresa was to be detained at the Incarnation. She had to obey the orders of her superior, however much it pained her not to be able to share the life of her nuns.

But meanwhile time was working for her, time which brings to men and things insight and maturity. The day came when a humble remark of the prisoner sufficed to change her jailer's mind. With all the humility of a subordinate nun, but at the same time with the superior assurance of one who has had intercourse with the powers of heaven, Theresa said to the provincial Salazar: "Look father, we are resisting the Holy Ghost." He surely did not wish to incur such a risk and gave Theresa permission to return to her convent. He even made it possible for her to take with her four other nuns who had come to embrace her views.

One morning in the winter of 1563 five barefoot nuns, wrapped in sackcloth, waded through the snow-covered streets of Ávila. Theresa de Cepeda returned with four new disciples to the convent of her choice. At St. Joseph's the four nuns who had lived there like orphaned children, welcomed her back with the jubilant exclamation: "Madre!" And from then on all her nuns called her la madre. For the world outside, however, Teresa de Cepeda became Teresa de Jesú. Her predicate of inherited nobility was replaced by a predicate of nobility by spiritual descent.

A short time later three additional virgins knocked at the door of the convent of St. Joseph and asked to be admitted into the ranks of the discalced nuns. Then, one day, the deserted street in front of the convent became the scene of an event which set all Ávila astir. A procession of fifteen festively decked-out carriages drew up in front of the modest building. Fourteen of them were occupied by handsome young caballeros, dressed in all the splendor of the Castilian nobility of the time. They were the sons of the wealthiest families of Ávila and formed the retinue of Doña María Dávila, the most popular beauty in town, who occupied the fifteenth carriage and had invited all her admirers to take part in this strange parade. She was dressed from head to toe in velvet and silk; her cheeks and lips were beautifully painted; her neck and her wrists were adorned with gold and precious stones. Never, never had she been more beautiful, more worthy of admiration, than now, when she stood up in her carriage, surveying the tense silence in the rows of her suitors. It was the thought of all of them that she would now, in this eccentric fashion, announce her final choice, and each one was filled with fear and hope alike. Once more she looked around with strangely steadied glances. Then she opened her crimsoned lips. "Farewell, farewell!" she said, and her eyes grew hard and solemn and looked far beyond the things she could see. "World, farewell!" The *caballeros* in their carriages did not find time to recover before Doña María had stepped down from her seat, and hastened to the door of the little convent where she knocked and disappeared never to return.

Inside she was received by Madre Theresa and her eleven nuns who conducted her in silence to the chapel. There, in front of the altar, the nuns took off her costly garments, her precious jewels, piece by piece, and dressed her in sackcloth and left her feet bare. Then brother Julian, the priest of the Discalced Carmelites of St. Joseph, took her vows. The following day the wealthy and respected Jose Dávila received a bundle to which this note was attached: "These are the belongings of your daughter María." It was signed: "María de Santa Jerónima, daughter of *la madre de* San José." The charming girl who had thus turned into a nun was to become one of the most reliable pillars of the discalced reform.

Theresa's dream had come true. She had longed for it, she had fought and suffered for it. But now it had been achieved. The house of silence was a reality. Charity was the only patron of her convent. Poverty was its builder, privation its cook and discipline its guardian. The tile-covered floors in the cells were table, chair and bed alike. The panes in the window frames were replaced by pieces of cloth. A revolving disk, the so-called *torno*, which was built into the wall, served to receive gifts of food. Whatever was placed there by charitable souls made up the daily fare of the nuns. At times there was a piece of cheese, a few eggs or a little bread, often just a few stale crusts, and then again the torso remained altogether empty. Whatever else the little community could not dispense with, had to be earned by spinning and needle work. The yield was not determined by value or price; it was whatever charity chose to give. The nuns merely put their work outside the convent gate, and the price was left to the discretion of the buyer. There was no parlor, no visiting hours, which could have shortened the working day. There were no gossiping nuns to interfere with prayer and contemplation.

Life was not easy for the inmates of St. Joseph. There was no security, and today none could know what the morrow might bring. And yet there were twelve nuns living there in happiness under the guidance of their cheerful superior. For the piety of the madre was of a cheerful kind. "God deliver us from sullen saints," said the prioress of St. Joseph's, and again and again she impressed upon her daughters her deep conviction: "A sad nun is a bad nun."

She imbued the convent with the spirit of her own cheerful piety, and when she had invited poverty to live with her and her nuns on the bare tiles of St. Joseph's, carefree contentment had moved in too. What the nuns did not have, they did not miss; and since they owned nothing, the urge to own could not enslave them to material things. Since the days of St. Francis, the Christian faith in God had never been so joyful, so jubilant.

At St. Joseph's Theresa had found for the first time a real home on earth. It lay on a narrow street in the Spanish town of Avila, but it lay also in the immediate neighborhood of heaven where she was often transported in rapturous ecstasies. When she returned to her nuns, it was no longer a fall to abysmal depths, as it had been at the Incarnation; she came back to her home as from a neighborly call.

For five years Theresa lived blissfully in the serene tranquility of her convent. But this period of contemplative happiness was only an interval of rest in the missionary's life ahead of her

The unexpected visit of John Baptist Rubeo, the Carmelite general, was the prelude to a new phase in Theresa's life. Rubeo had been ordered by the Pope to inspect the Carmelite monasteries and convents all over Spain. At the Council of Trent measures to strengthen the tottering church had been the major topic for discussion. The prevailing view had been that it would first of all be necessary to put a stop to the laxness of life in the monastic orders. And this was the purpose of Rubeo's tour of inspection. Wherever he had been, he had met with difficulties and opposition, for after a century of the mitigated rule a great many abuses had come to be considered as established rights.

At St. Joseph's Rubeo found to his great surprise that all the reforms, which he had been trying in vain to promote elsewhere, were here fully in force. St. Theresa had anticipated the decrees of the Council of Trent and had implemented their recommendations long before anyone else had thought of formulating them. Thus it came to pass that Rubeo, before leaving again, gave not only permission for additional houses to be founded in the spirit of St. Joseph's, but actually encouraged and admonished Theresa to extend her activities.

One morning in August 1567, a strange caravan passed through the gates of the town of Ávila. It consisted of four covered wagons with wooden wheels and no springs. In the first wagon sat a veiled woman—*la madre*—, in the second and third some of her nuns; the fourth and last carried the belongings of the travelers and their holy vessels. Father Julian, the ordained priest of St. Joseph's, rode on a donkey next to the wagon of the madre, and muleteers, in the colorful Spanish clothes of their profession, walked along, left and right, with the teams. It was scorching hot. The road was bad, in places almost impassable. The stubborn mules paid little attention to the encouraging shouts of *arre! arre!* of their drivers, who had to have recourse to their most powerful Castilian oaths, and after the first five miles would have liked nothing better than to give in to the mules and turn back. Medina, the destination of the little caravan, was still seventy miles off. Theresa, who wanted to reach her goal at all costs, had nothing to say to pacify the muleteers but that God had ordered this trip and that they should keep going for His sake. At first her words were drowned in the general swearing. But before long those tough men were gently walking along, listening to Theresa who was talking to them as a mother talks to her children.

In Medina del Campo the little caravan of poverty was anything but welcome. The firmly established Carmelite and Augustinian monks looked askance at the intruders, whose postulates of asceticism might put their lives of comfortable piety in an unfavorable perspective, and whose complete destitution would doubtless absorb much of the charitable potential of Medina's fifty thousand souls. All sorts of obstacles were put in the way of Theresa's plans for a new convent. The only house offered her as shelter for her nuns was a dilapidated building with a leaking roof and cracks in the walls. No one could recall ever having seen it occupied, and even tramps and vagrants would not stay there, because they could always find something better.

The following morning the townspeople of Medina were awakened by the sound of a new bell which came out of the old house and announced the first mass of the Discalced. That night a few eggs lay in front of the convent gate, and soon there was bread and cheese to feed the nuns. A few days later, right after the matins, St. Joseph's resounded with the loud noise of busy hammering. Workmen had started the job of repairing the leaks in the roof and of filling the cracks in the walls. In the course of the morning a van drew up in front of the building, and tables and wooden benches were unloaded. No one had called in the carpenters and roofers; no one had ordered the tables and benches. Charity had sent them to the home of the discalced nuns. A farmer's wife came to implore the nuns to pray for her daughter who was dangerously ill. A few weeks later the girl, who had recovered, came in herself and stayed as a novice. The people of Medina had sided with the nuns; but for the present the angered monks persisted in their hostility.

Then one day the *madre* was informed that two monks wished to speak to her. She found two calced Carmelite monks, who made an extremely incongruous pair. The one was a man of mature age of powerful build, a giant in monk's garb; the other a youth of some twenty-four years, of small stature, barely reaching up to his partner's chest, and of such slender and delicate build that there was something ethereal about him, a boy in the garb of a monk.

The stately figure was the prior of the calced Carmelites of Medina, Antonio de Heredia; his youthful companion was Friar John, one of the monks of his monastery. The prior spoke for both of them. The example of the discalced nuns, he said, had aroused in them the desire to lead a similarly pious life. By giving them her rules — they had thought — she, Theresa, might help them in their plan to establish a discalced monastery.

This unexpected request fulfilled for Theresa, through a gift of unsolicited grace, what she had not dared to hope for in her boldest dreams: the possibility of extending her work to the male branch of the Carmelites and thus of imbuing the entire order with her ideas of reform and restoration. She consented with joy in her heart. When she looked once more at the strange pair, her innate sense of humor could not repress the roguish observation: "Blessed be the Lord, for I have a friar and a half for the foundation of my new monastery." But after her first more exhaustive conversation with the two Carmelite monks, she recognized that the half-friar would be considerably more important for the propagation of her ideas of monastic reform than the venerable giant, the converted prior of the calced monks, and that this frail youth in a monk's cowl was sent to her by God and would become her equal as partner in her life's work. For Friar John was no less a person than the Carmelite monk, whom the history of the saints remembers as St. John of the Cross, San Juan de la Cruz, one of the most gifted, most immaculate mystic poets of world literature.

He was of peasant stock, the son of a linen weaver, quite unorthodox, it is true, with his visions befalling him during his walks through forests and fields, and the mystic hymns which he composed. He had turned his back on the world and sought the safety of a God-pleasing life in a Carmelite monastery. But in the worldly bustle of contemporary monasticism he had not found the answer to his quest and was convinced that salvation could only be attained in the spirit of Theresa's reform.

He contributed to her work his enthusiasm arising from a deep longing for true piety, his faith strengthened by mystical experience, and the quietude of his heart which had its source in heaven.

Theresa and John were of different worldly lineage, of different sex and of different age; yet they were both of the same spiritual lineage, of the same spiritual sex and had the same spiritual maturity. They both were mystics, poets, saints. What distinguished them outwardly, was eliminated by an inner identity of purpose and ideal. Their work was enlivened by the same spirit, the same holiness. It was destined to be a unique kind of work, for the quietude of their hearts and the mysticism of their minds united these two visionaries in practical activity and made of stillness and vision an earthly reality.

The first monastery of discalced friars was set up in Duruelo, not far from Salamanca. The former prior of the calced Carmelites, Antonio de Heredia, now Antonio de Jesú, was also the first discalced prior; but it was Friar John's spirit that pervaded the organization of the new institution, that formulated the principles of its discipline and held absolute sway over all its concerns. The building of this first discalced monastery was a dungeonlike structure the furnishings of which consisted of two stones and two bundles of hay serving John and Antonio as pillows and beds. In course of time the monastery of the discalced friars at Duruelo grew in size. But nothing in its organization was changed. Only the number of pillows of stone and the number of bundles of hay were increased in proportion to the increased number of friars, of austere fasters and quiet worshipers.

Medina del Campo, the first stage of Theresa's reform work, signified thus not only the first foundation of a discalced convent outside of Ávila but also the first successful move in her comprehensive campaign for the reform of both the male and female branches of the Carmelite order. It signified—something that had never been heard of before—success and fame for a Spanish woman. Here a woman appeared in the limelight of public attention who not only had broken the ban barring all women from participation in public activities but who had become the founder of an institution for men, in which men of all ages and nations were to participate.

One after the other new convents and monasteries of the reform grew up under the creative hand of this indefatigable missionary. Theresa no longer had to fight for the consent of the communities; she no longer had to be content with dilapidated old homes. From everywhere she received letters requesting her to honor this place or that by the foundation of a discalced convent. The people vied with each other for the privilege of placing at her disposal houses and homes in which her nuns could live their life of pious contemplation. And now, when the fame of this popular saint had reached the court of Philip II, the nobility too did not wish to remain in the background but was eager to take an active part in the reform. The first of the rich and noble, who could pride herself with having dedicated a house of poverty, was Theresa's old acquaintance, the once disconsolate widow Luise de la Cerda.

When the princess Ana Eboli learned that her best-hated rival, the duchess de la Cerda, had stolen a march upon her, she decided to overtrump her and not just to put one of her houses in Pastrana at the disposal of the saintly reformer but to take the veil and move herself into the convent of poverty. She left her sumptuous palace, took leave from her one hundred costly robes and five hundred costly lace mantillas, donned an artistically mended garb of sackcloth, hired a rickety peasant cart, drove, accompanied by two chambermaids, to the house which she herself had dedicated to the reform, and announced that she intended to live there henceforth as a discalced Carmelite nun.

She insisted that her chambermaids be admitted to the novitiate too. Then the "newly baked chambernuns" were ordered to unpack her trunks. Her cell was filled with dozens of carefully patched Carmelite habits of various cuts and patterns, each one for a different occasion in her proposed career as a discalced nun. There was one for the matins, another one for vespers; one for the kitchen, one for contemplation, and a very special one for high mass in honor of the holy martyrs.

Her meals, carefully prepared for a discalced faster, were brought over from her palace. She insisted on keeping her predicate of nobility and received visitors from outside whenever she pleased. From the first the nuns and even the prioress were ordered around by her, for she saw no reason why she should not be the mistress of them all.

Theresa was just occupied with the organization of a new convent in Alba de Tormes, when the prioress of Pastrana wrote to her in despair about the antics of princess Eboli. At once she rushed to Pastrana, for what was going on there was even more important than the establishment of a new house of the reform. It concerned the integrity and purity of the reform as a whole. No gift of money, no donation of houses, however liberal, could confound her in the pursuit of her ideal of pious living. And when she arrived in Pastrana and stood face to face with the princess to discuss the situation that had developed, she was not a grateful protégée talking to a generous patron but a determined protagonist of the ideal of poverty fighting the arrogance of a presumptuous representative of wealth. A displeased superior reprimanded an unruly nun, who had dared to violate the rules of silence, poverty and humility. The princess was accustomed to order, not to obey, and in a rage she exclaimed: "This is my house, and I demand that my orders be obeyed!" But Theresa replied: "This is the house of the Lord, and I demand that His orders be obeyed!" The princess had nothing more to say.

She left within the hour. She took her chambermaids and her trunks with her and vowed vengeance upon the ungrateful nuns. In the eyes of the faithful, however, Theresa's fearless demeanor in front of the powerful princess strengthened her reputation and that of the reform she stood for. She had proved that she knew not only how to found an order of poverty but also how to defend it.

The Carmelites of the mitigated rule watched with growing concern the success of mother Theresa's movement. The houses of the discalced increased in quick succession. The reform had begun to affect the male branch of the Carmelite order as well. It was no longer the convent of the Incarnation alone but the entire order, that was in danger. As a Carmelite nun Theresa was still subject to the jurisdiction of the order, although as a saint, whose name was known and admired throughout Spain, she was proof against a direct attack. It was no longer possible, as it had been, to recall her to the Incarnation and have a jury of nuns pass judgment on, but it was possible to paralyze her work by giving her a position of honor at the mother convent. The Carmelites of the mitigated rule knew how to lay the trap of honorary rewards.

The Carmelite provincial made Theresa the prioress of the Incarnation. Her task was to remedy the prevailing laxness and to lead the nuns back to a stricter form of devotion. What a triumph! What wonderful recognition of her organizational skill! What satisfaction to be placed as prioress over the nuns who had once passed judgment against her! But mainly, what splendid opportunity of taking her away, for three entire years, from her work for the reform and of keeping her imprisoned at the Incarnation!

At first Theresa was shocked by the assignment. She looked through the intrigue which was hiding behind the mask of honor and recognition. At the height of success she was forced to abandon her work as a reformer in order to function as the prioress of a convent of the mitigated rule, where the nuns were protesting in open rebellion against her appointment.

But when Theresa started on her way back to the Incarnation, she did so not only because she was bound by her vows to render obedience to the order, but she meant to devote herself wholeheartedly to the solution of the task that had been entrusted to her. She knew that this newest assignment was a trap of her enemies, but she had really resolved to serve God, she must serve Him, also in the trap of her enemies, with undiminished ardor. She now had but one end in view: to lead the "poor things" of the Incarnation, who had once been her fellow nuns, back on the one and only road to God. Misfortune turned into a new task, and in order to cope with it effectively, she appointed St. John of the Cross as father confessor of the Incarnation, for in him the nuns would have a spiritual leader after her mind, of her humility and quietude of soul.

The nuns of the Incarnation received her in a spirit of undisguised hostility. She was greeted with insults and accusations. But after the provincial had confirmed the finality of his decision, the anger of the nuns turned into apprehension, for they feared the retaliatory strictness of their new superior. The first chapter day, when the prioress was to make her speech of acceptance, a worried file of nuns moved into the refectory. But what a surprise was awaiting them there! The rostrum, which they were wont to see reserved for the prioress, was occupied by a statue of the Holy Virgin. Theresa was kneeling before it. When she arose to speak to the nuns, she pointed to the Virgin and said: "This is your new prioress. Her orders you and I will have to obey. I have only been appointed to lead you and be your guide in obedience."

As if by magic, all fear had vanished from the hearts of the nuns, and also all indignation and all hate. Before long the nuns of the Incarnation asked Theresa that the parlor be abolished; they took up the practice of mental prayer in the quietude of their cells and patterned their lives more and more after the rules of the discalced.

Thus the ruse of the mitigation turned out badly for the instigators themselves. Now Theresa had on her side a convent of the mitigated rule, where calced nuns lived in the spirit of the discalced reform. Yet the price her adversaries had to pay was not too high. They profited by the years which Theresa had to spend at the Incarnation and succeeded in inducing Rubeo, the general of the order, to change his mind about her; they won over the Holy See and began to undermine Theresa's reputation in Spain by well-organized calumniatory propaganda. While she and St. John of the Cross guided the nuns of the Incarnation to a life of quiet devotion, messengers were dispatched to Piacenza where the general of the Carmelites had his seat; emissaries were sent to Rome to influence the Pope; visitors of the church, who favored the reform, were replaced by hostile ones; discalced nuns were stirred up against the madre, and the monks were warned against a woman who brazenly usurped the rule over men. When Theresa had completed her term of office at the Incarnation and came out to resume her interrupted work for the reform, she immediately came up against the solid ranks of the opposition which was all set for an attack of well-aimed blows.

Excess of zeal on the part of Theresa's friends had played into the hands of her enemies. The most enthusiastic of her followers, Father Gracian, proved also to be the most harmful. She had met him while setting up a new monastery at Veas. He was her junior by thirty years, bald and stocky, well-versed in theological matters but totally unversed in dealings with men; he was devout and filled with true goodness of heart but unbridled, obstinate and aggressive in the pursuit of his ends. He was a man with many excellent traits but also with an equal number of faults. At first Theresa was blinded by his enthusiasm and saw only his virtues. She installed him as prior of her monastery at Veas and not only entrusted to him the task of organizing additional houses of the reform but even made him her own father confessor.

In his fervent desire to serve the *madre* Gracian set out immediately to organize discalced monasteries at Granada and Penuela. But Granada and Penuela were in Andalusia, and this provided the calced Carmelites with an excellent argument against the reform. When the general of the order Rubeo had given his consent for the establishment of new houses, no mention had been made of Andalusia, and thus the reform had overstepped its rights. The foundations in Andalusia were illegal.

Another friend of the reform, the papal visitator Vargas, fanned up the hatred of Theresa's adversaries still further by choosing amongst all possible choices the discalced Gracian as his delegate in Andalusia, so that the Carmelites of the mitigated rule came to be placed under the jurisdiction of a Carmelite of the reform.

This local incident was seized upon by the calced partisans elsewhere and was made the cause for convoking a general chapter of the order at Piacenza, where Rubeo saw fit to withdraw his protection from Theresa in order to calm the excited minds. The chapter voted unanimously in favor of closing the new houses in Andalusia. In case there should be any sort of resistance, it would be dealt with in a spirit of ruthless determination. To avoid every possibility of unwelcome interference, Rubeo obtained from the Pope the promise that Vargas would be recalled and that the Portuguese Carmelite Fray Jerónimo Tostado, a reliable opponent of the reform, would be appointed to take his place. All this assured the liquidation of the reform in Andalusia, but it did not assure what was really the main purpose of the mitigation, the ousting of the head of the reform, of Theresa herself. For that something more seemed needed; a scandal which would set all Spain astir with excitement.

Theresa enjoyed the reputation of a saint, and this reputation had to be undermined. The mere fact that her life and demeanor was beyond reproach, did not disturb the ill will of her enemies. If there were no facts, calumny had to be relied upon to do the job. And calumny did the job, and did it well.

Gracian had committed grave blunders, yet Theresa refused to relieve him of his post. She even kept him as her father confessor and had him accompany her on her trips. Why did she cling so stubbornly to this criminally stupid monk? Calumny replied with ingenuous cunning: Obviously because he is her lover, because she wants to confess her love to him, because she needs him on her outings of love. Wherever Theresa arrived to found new homes of the reform, slanderous rumor had moved in ahead and waited for her at the city gates and interfered with the execution of her plans.

The next trip took her to Seville. Ten of her nuns and Father Gracian accompanied her. For ten days they had to endure the scorching heat of Southern Spain. Their food was made up of a few salted sardines. For miles around there was not a drop of water to be had. Worn out by thirst and fatigue Theresa broke down in a roadside inn. Drunken ruffians ridiculed the nuns and threatened to attack them, when a band of *caballeros* with drawn swords appeared on the scene and rescued the nuns in a regular little skirmish. Finally Theresa and her group could proceed on their way. After many hardships they arrived in Seville.

This was the city of gold. It was the city where the ships from Mexico and Peru arrived with their precious cargoes. The inhabitants were interested in nothing but gold. Gold was their god and love of life their religion. Here a woman who preached poverty, renunciation and silence could not expect to be welcomed with open arms. It was but natural that the rumor of her amours had fallen on fertile ground. All of Seville was against her. Even the old archbishop, a good and pious Christian, was so prejudiced against her that he not only withheld his dispensation for a new convent of the reform but even refused to grant her an audience. Still Theresa's enemies were not satisfied. Her mere presence in Seville was a scandal, and the archbishop, they felt, had better order Theresa to leave the city immediately. It was this excess of zeal, which wrecked the whole intrigue.

The archbishop summoned the "impostor" to inform her of the order of expulsion, but by the time she left, he had recognized the saint in her, had permitted her to found monasteries and convents and had assured her of his wholehearted support. When the reformed convent of St. Joseph of Seville was consecrated, the archbishop came in person at the head of a solemn procession, and when Theresa was about to kneel down to receive his fatherly blessing, he prevented her, knelt down himself before her and asked her to bless him with the blessing of saintliness. Together with the archbishop a great many of the faithful of Seville went over to Theresa's side, and many a daughter of many a wealthy merchant left her home of comfort to find refuge in the convent of poverty of the discalced nuns.

This unexpected turn of events roused the anger of the calced Carmelites to red-hot fury. They were immediately ready for the next blow against the hated reformer and felt certain that this time they would finish her off once and for all. They had succeeded in smuggling one of their adherents as a novice into the convent of the reform. One day this "discalced" sister escaped from St. Joseph's and spread the shocking story that the *madre* flogged her nuns and heard their confessions of sin as though she were their father confessor. This latter charge was particularly grave, for it implied illuminism, the most abject crime of heresy in the eyes of the Inquisition.

One morning, when Father Gracian appeared at the gates of St. Joseph's, mounted guards kept him from entering. Mother Theresa, about whom he inquired, had already been taken into custody. Theresa's case was a special one, for it concerned not only Seville and the Carmelites but Rome and the royal court at Madrid as well. The Inquisition spared no trouble. It re-examined all previous charges, including the ugly accusations of princess Eboli, for it wished to determine once and for all whether Theresa was a desirable reformer in the spirit of the resolutions of the Council of Trent or an infamous heretic.

Quiet and unafraid the accused stood before her judges not uttering a word in her own defense. She looked at the Grand Inquisitor, but she did not see his grim face; she saw only the benevolent face of the Lord who was sitting in judgment over her in heaven. And the Lord looked angrily at her accusers in the judgment hall, but when His eyes beheld her, the accused, he smiled encouragingly. Theresa was carried away in one of her raptures. But when it was over, when she had returned to the judgment hall and faced the Grand Inquisitor again, then it seemed that her vision had become an earthly reality. The Grand Inquisitor looked angrily at her accusers and turning around to look at her, he smiled encouragingly, exactly as the Lord had done in her vision, and said: "You are acquitted of all charges. What you have done and what you do is in accordance with the will of God. Go then and continue your work."

But still there were the calced Carmelites on earth who wanted to defend their comfortable ways of serving God against the dangers of the reform. And just when their campaign of calumny seemed to have definitely failed through Theresa's acquittal by the Inquisition, they suddenly received powerful reinforcements. The Portuguese Tostado, the delegate of the Carmelite chapter at Piacenza, arrived in Spain to put into effect the resolutions which the chapter had passed against Theresa. He brought with him various authorizations which revived the hopes of the partisans of the mitigated rule. Now it seemed again as though their plans might come true after all.

Theresa was forbidden to continue her work. Tostado ordered her to retire to a convent of her choice and to abstain from founding new houses of the reform. "It was like sending me to a prison," she remarked. She chose St. Joseph's at Toledo. Father Gracian, who had hastily convoked a chapter of the discalced, was arrested by Tostado's order. Otherwise too everything seemed to take a favorable turn for the mitigation. Ormaneto, the papal nuncio in Spain, who was very well disposed toward the discalced reform, died suddenly, and the calced Carmelites succeeded in inducing the Pope to appoint in his stead Sega, the bishop of Piacenza. The new nuncio was equipped for his office with every conceivable prejudice against the discalced. He called Theresa a restless creature and summed up his views regarding her in these terms: "She is a disobedient, contumacious woman, who promulgates pernicious doctrines under the pretense of devotion, who left her cloister against the orders of her superiors, who is ambitious and teaches theology as though she were a doctor of the Church, in contempt of the teaching of St. Paul who commanded women not to teach." Whatever Tostado decreed in the name of the Carmelite order, was sanctioned by Sega in the name of the Pope.

When Theresa retired to Toledo, various pamphlets against her had already been put in circulation. But she was inured to distress and disappointments and did not take the matter to heart. "I am amused by all this," she said. "God forgive these people!

However, it is best if they make so many accusations at once, as no one can believe all of them."

But then something happened which even Theresa could not take coolly but which forced her to think of immediate countermeasures. St. John of the Cross was taken away from her, and that in a manner which defied all laws of human decency. One day he disappeared, kidnaped and hidden by the calced Carmelites. Theresa's desperate efforts to find him were all in vain.

After the crushing verdict which the papal nuncio had passed against Theresa and which had meanwhile been spread among the clergy all over Spain, there was no one ready to lend her a helping hand in her search. She was faced with a united front of conspirators. Then, following a quick impulse, she turned to Philip II. He was not only the king of Spain but at the time the "most powerful man of Christendom," and his word carried no less weight than that of the pontiff at Rome. If she could win his support, she had triumphed over all her enemies, including the papal nuncio.

As a skilled diplomat, who was keenly alive to the struggle for power among the great, she composed a letter to the king, describing in heartfelt terms the intrigues against the reform and the abduction of the most God fearing of her followers and imploring the king to act as her protector on earth. Philip II answered without delay. He knew Theresa's *Vida* and kept his copy of it as a precious possession in a special box, the key to which he carried with him wherever he went. In quiet nights the *Vida* had often afforded him the solace and edification which his soul craved. He, who knew the story of her life, who had read the account of her visions in trustful admiration, needed no further proof to be convinced of her purity and of the injustice of the cause of her persecutors.

He was used to an environment of fawning courtiers and intriguing dignitaries of the church and was fascinated by the idea of meeting a saint. He sent a special courier to invite Theresa to an audience at court.

The trip to Madrid Theresa undertook again in her springless cart. A snowstorm detained her for a few days in Valladolid, and in mid-December, 1577, she arrived at the king's residence. The most powerful ruler of the world and the representative of a realm which is not of this world came face to face with each other. It was an audience, which deviated also in its outer form from the usual etiquette at court. Theresa opened the conversation by quoting the contemptuous remarks the papal nuncio had made about her. "Sire," she said, "you are thinking now, so this is that disobedient, contumacious woman who promulgates pernicious doctrines under the pretense of devotion." But the king seemed to be of a different opinion, for he relaxed unexpectedly in his sternly majestic bearing and made, as Theresa described it, "the most courteous bow I ever saw."

Her petition and his reply were disposed of in a very few words. After she had presented her case and asked him for his support, Philip inquired: "Is that all you want?" "I have asked a great deal," Theresa replied, and the king assured her: "Then be at peace, for all shall be as you wish." Then the king spoke as one whom the presence of a saint makes deeply aware of the wretchedness of his position on the throne of the world.

When Philip set out to fulfill his promise, he did so as a proud autocrat who resented the machinations which a foreigner, the Portuguese Tostado, had permitted himself on Spanish soil against a Spanish saint. He simply ordered this undesirable alien to leave the country. When Sega asked for an audience, he had to listen to a string of stern reprimands. The very first words the king addressed to the representative of the Pope were these: "I am aware of the hostility of the mitigated friars to the reform, and this looks bad, for the discalced lead austere lives of perfection. See that you favor virtue, for people tell me that you are no friend of the discalced." He demanded that Sega authorize immediately an impartial investigation of the reform. The Roman diplomat did not relish the prospect of friction with the most Christian monarch and consented forthwith. The impartial investigation demonstrated beyond reasonable doubt the absolute untenability of all charges against Theresa and the reform. It convinced even Sega that he and the Holy Father had been misled by a malevolent opposition. And then the Holy See itself stopped once and for all, by a radical decree, the intrigues of the calced against the discalced Carmelites. Pope Gregory XIII issued a bull which established the reform by setting up a separate order of discalced Carmelites. Thus Theresa's movement attained independence, and there was nothing that could interfere with its further growth.

Then too, Theresa recovered also St. John of the Cross. He returned, steeled by the martyrdom of prison, transfigured in the eyes of all Christians by the miracle of his escape. The calced Carmelites, who had abducted him, kept him for nine months locked up in a narrow chamber inside the wall of one of their monasteries. It was six feet wide and ten feet long and was dimly lighted through a grilled opening which looked out on a fortified passageway. He had one or two rags to sleep on, and his food consisted of two or three crusts of stale bread and half a glass of water, which were given him, at first daily but after a while only twice every week. When he was still not ready to abjure his faith in the reform, the monks thought of even sterner measures and took him every evening to the refectory to flog him. His emaciated figure, stripped to the waist, knelt in the center of the room, while the calced friars, armed with sticks and clubs, walked around in a circle, taking turns at beating him with all their strength, until his bleeding and lacerated body sank unconscious to the floor. Night after night the flogging went on, but St. John of the Cross did not abjure. "Senseless block!" his tormentors shouted in impotent rage, but he looked at them steadfast and silent, for all this torture was for him but one of the stations of his *imitatio Christi*.

And after the ordeal was over, when his pitifully maltreated body, rather dead than alive, lay again in the dark hole of the cloister wall, then suddenly another life arose in him which was not vulnerable to human hate. For it was a life that turned into song, into verse and stanza, and in it the torment he had suffered was changed into sweetness. And this song of sweetness carried a tone which rang above life and pain in God. He did not want to lose it and memorized it again and again until it was indelibly impressed upon his mortal mind. For seventeen nights the friars flogged him. Every night the flogging added a new stanza to his song. Those were the seventeen nights which gave to the world the seventeen stanzas of the "Spiritual Canticle" of St. John of the Cross, the most sublime and at the same time the most passionate mystical hymn of Spanish literature, of the literature of the world.

The tormentors were thinking of new forms of torture, but the stanzas of divine passion had been brought to perfection. A radiant vision penetrated the darkness of St. John's prison. It emanated from the robe of light of the Holy Virgin who appeared to him and ordered him to get up and leave. Through the grilled opening? Over walls and roof tops? St. John did not query, he did not wonder. He obeyed the order of the vision of light.

His lacerated body got up with athletic strength. His tired arms could bend the heavy rods with perfect ease. Two threadbare rags were fashioned into a rope and St. John slid down over the passageway to the wall below. He then let himself fall. He was not hurt. He landed on a garbage pile, he did not know where. A dog that had been trying to find something to eat there ran off into the darkness. John followed him. The dog jumped over a wall. John climbed over too and found himself in a courtyard. He heard the voice of a woman. Going in the direction from where it came he reached a house and entered. It was the convent of the discalced nuns. And while the calced friars pursued him with lanterns, clubs and shouts of anger, he lay hidden and cared-for in the infirmary of the convent. The dreamer of heaven had withstood the trials of the world and took up again his place at Theresa's side.

Theresa was sixty-three years of age. Four more years, that was all that was granted her to extend and strengthen her work, the last years, as she wrote herself, "of an aged woman, good for little now, very old and weary . . ." But then she added: "Yet my desires are still vigorous." To the ills of her younger years were added now the infirmities of old age. Overcome by a fainting spell, she fell down the stairs on her way to mass on Christmas day at St. Joseph's in Ávila and broke her left arm. From then on she was no longer able to dress and undress without help. For a while she was almost completely paralyzed, and when she recovered, she could not move about without a cane. Her stomach kept hardly any food. Heart attacks of ever increasing frequency kept her periodically confined to bed. "I am nothing more than a poor old hag," she wrote to Father Gracian.

And yet, the last years of her life were filled with activity. She kept up her travels. She feared no hardship and shunned no toil. During these years she was indefatigably at work to give her reform firmness and permanence. She visited again her older foundations. She examined and inspected, she improved and corrected. She established a number of new houses of the reform. She drafted a well-thought-out constitution for her order and convoked the first chapter general of the discalced Carmelites.

Illness was only the dark background against which her radiant figure stood out the more brightly. While her ills had once been the earthly source of her heavenly visions, they were now the touchstone which demonstrated the mastery of her will over all human frailty.

During a tour of inspection she was seized by a paralytic fit at Malaga. But no sooner had she recovered halfway than she continued her trip. In Toledo she suffered another attack. Her companions implored her to rest for a few days at least. But she would not listen and insisted: "I am so used to suffer that I can well endure the trip."

The following morning she went on to Segovia and thence, trembling with exhaustion and always in her springless cart, to Vallalolid where she collapsed. But still she went on to Salamanca and back to Ávila. She paid no attention to a grave heart attack and started out again for Palencia where she wanted to establish a new convent. In Palencia her condition grew worse, and she herself had to admit: "I am very ill and it is thought that I cannot live." But once more she left with her little caravan in order to establish at Burgos a last convent to the greater glory of her order. Neither her weakness nor the warning words of her friends, who tried to tell her what great hardships such a trip in late winter would entail, could sway her decision,

Beset with pains but unshakable in her determination and filled with joy at the thought of her new enterprise, she had herself lifted into her cart. She cheerfully ordered the muleteers to start. Torrential rains marking the turn from winter to spring had flooded the roads. The carts drove axle-deep through the mud and finally were stuck altogether. The travelers had to leave the vehicles behind and try to get through on foot. If it had not been for the sick and aged madre who plodded on cheerfully, leaning on the arms of two of her nuns, comforting and encouraging her little group with humorous or edifying remarks, they all, like their carts, would have been lost in the mire. With almost superhuman efforts they finally fought their way through. At a point, from where the towers of Burgos were visible, they reached the Arlanzon river, which the rains had swelled to a wild torrent. The bridge had been carried away, but the madre would not turn back, especially now when she saw in the distance the outlines of the home of the Cid Campeador. "Come what may," she said cheerfully. "If you faint on your way, if you die on the road, if the world is destroyed, all is well if you reach your goal." And when she saw that some of her companions were still undecided, she added confidently: "The Lord who has helped us through the mud will also help us across this river." With these words she went ahead into the icy water. Her determination inspired the wavering nuns. One after the other they followed her into the water. In midstream she slipped. A wave swept her down the river. She did not scream, she was not frightened, she merely asked the Lord in her need: "Oh, Lord, why do you put such difficulties in our way?" Then the Lord appeared over the water and replied: "It is thus I treat my friends." And Theresa, never at a loss for an answer, said with her characteristic sense of humor: "Ah, my Lord, that is why you have so few."

The nuns meanwhile stood helpless and lost in the middle of the river. Then of a sudden they saw to their joy and surprise the figure of their *madre* waving to them from the other side. How they got across, they could not explain later on. All they remembered was that they had followed the call of their *madre*. That same night they reached Burgos, and the following morning they began work on setting up a new convent. It was Theresa's last foundation, and she called it the "Glorious St. Joseph of Burgos."

If the trip to Burgos had not killed her, she felt certain she could also survive the trip to Alba de Tormes. But in Alba a hemorrhage of the lungs forced her down, and this time forever. The first week she adhered strictly, in spite of her illness, to the convent rules she herself had laid down. She observed the hours of prayer and the fast, she performed all her domestic duties, but finally she recognized that her task now was not to master life but to triumph over death. And more cheerfully, more courageously, more determinedly than she had fulfilled the tasks of her life, she now accepted the task of dying. She was not inexperienced in the art of dying, and death itself, the goal of this last journey, had always been familiar to her. In her mystic experience of death, in her ecstatic poems of death, she had often anticipated its coming. For her, whose life here below had been lived simultaneously in this world and the next, death had no sting. For her, death was but the threshold which she crossed to live henceforth and forever in the realm of Life Eternal.

"Oh death, oh death," she had exclaimed a long time ago. "I know not who should be afraid of you since you are filled with life itself. What happiness to think that we are not going to a strange country but to our own." And in one of her most beautiful poems, "The Yearning of the Soul for a Reunion with God" she wrote:

All my life reposes here
In the certitude of death,
For this trust holds promises
To rejoin us life's own sphere;
Death, you source of life—appear,
All my hopes in you imply,
I'll die because I do not die.

Franciscan was the cheerfulness of her acceptance of life, but Franciscan was also the seriousness of her acceptance of death. To the last it remained her great endeavor to do justice to her mission in the world, and when her nuns were assembled around her deathbed, she turned to them and said: "For the love of God I beg that you will take great care with the keeping of the Rule and Constitutions, and pay no attention to the bad example that this wicked nun has given you, and pardon me for it." Then she turned to the other side and said to her Master: "Oh my Lord, the longed-for hour has come at last, and my soul rejoices in abiding with you forever."

The last nine hours of her life on earth she spent in a coma. Between nine and ten o'clock at night she died on the fourth of October, 1582. According to the calendar of the saints it was the day of St. Francis of Assisi. For the world it was the eve of the inauguration of the Gregorian calendar.

Her soul had finally passed into God's eternal quietude, but her body continued to belong to the restlessness of the earth. After she had been allowed to rest for nine months in her tomb at Alba, she again found herself on a springless peasant cart moving along the rough roads of Spain in the direction toward Ávila. This time the body of the saint obeyed the command of Father Gracian, the general of the order of the discalced Carmelites.

A satyrs' play appended to the sublime tragedy of a great life, that is in sum what this trip was like. Theresa had died on her last tour of inspection in Alba de Tormes. She had died in Alba and was interred in Alba. She was born in Ávila and had been the prioress of a convent in Ávila. Scarcely had the news of miracle-working powers in her body reached Ávila when a violent dispute broke out between Alba and Ávila as to which of the two held the better claim to the earthly remains of the saint. Gracian decided in favor of Ávila. Not only because it was there that she had come into the world but also because it was there that the Lord had revealed Himself to her for the first time, so that Ávila was the birthplace of her sainthood as well as of the reform. But Alba de Tormes was in the domain of the powerful house of the dukes of Alba, and they considered the body of the saint as part of their ducal treasure. The people of Ávila had to proceed under the cover of great secrecy if they wanted to get hold of the body. Theresa must be stolen.

Gracian had taken the Carmelite prioress at Alba into his confidence, and she, in order to forestall every possible interference, had all her nuns take part in an early morning choral service. While the nuns were singing, their miracle-working saint was removed from her tomb, loaded on a cart and sent off to Ávila.

No sooner had the body been interred in Ávila than it began to work miracles. They were kept strictly secret because the ducal house of the Albas must not hear about them. Also the subsequent exhumation of the body, which was undertaken by a special delegation of churchmen, took place behind closed doors, and all the participants had to vow absolute silence. But in spite of all vows the whole town of Ávila knew the following day that the body, when it was removed from its coffin, had shown no signs of decomposition and that one of its hands was stretched out, clearly as a gesture of blessing which she meant to bestow upon her native town. It took exactly as long as it takes a mounted messenger to get from Ávila to Alba, before the nuns at Alba were informed that the tomb before which they mourned and prayed was empty and that the body of their saint stretched out its blessing hand over the town of Ávila. Out of fear of the duchess of Alba the prioress ordered her nuns to preserve absolute silence in this matter. A young lay sister, however, who was working in the kitchen, listened at the door, baked a birthday cake for the ducal patroness, and baked into it a little note in which the whole story of the stolen body and the miracles it had worked in Ávila was reported in full.

The duchess was touched by the simple gift of her devout nuns. She cut the cake with her own ducal hand but got into a frenzy of rage when she read the message of the baked-in note. She forgot her birthday party and all her guests and rushed from her palace out into the street and, running in the direction of the convent, she kept screaming in pitiful lament: "They have stolen my saint! They have stolen my Santa Teresa!" What infamous wrong, crying to high heaven, had been done her! To be sure, Theresa was born in Ávila, but she had died in Alba, and from Alba she had ascended to heaven. Theresa's body was the rightful property of Alba. The duchess of Alba need not tolerate such infamous thievery. She dispatched an express courier to the pope in Rome, requesting him to right the wrong that Alba had suffered. The ducal house of the Albas was a powerful pillar of Roman might. The pope ordered the body to be returned. In order to forestall every possible interference, it was necessary to proceed under the cover of great secrecy. Theresa's body must be stolen again. One night, when the nuns, the bishop and the whole town were fast asleep, a covered wagon rumbled through the city gate of Ávila. It carried Theresa's body back to Alba.

But under the high altar of the church at Alba, where Theresa's body was now entombed, there was no final rest for it yet. Again and again the tomb was opened by special commissions charged to ascertain that her body was really unaffected by mortal decomposition. And soon the news of her miracle-working powers attracted devout thieves who did not shrink back from plundering her tomb.

Besides this comedy of errors, however, country and church were to bestow more dignified honors on the saint of the discalced reform. The Spanish Cortes and the king of Spain appealed together to Pope Urban VIII, who then declared St. Theresa, jointly with St. James, a patron of Spain. Meanwhile the process of her beatification was well underway. In the year 1614, seventy galleys of the Genoese fleet, under the command of Lord High Admiral Don Carter Porin, arrived at the port of Seville to deliver the decree of beatification of the Seraphic Theresa. Eight years later, forty years after her death, the seraphic *madre* was finally canonized together with Ignatius of Loyola and Francis Xavier.

Among the names of those who supported Theresa's beatification are not only Christian potentates and dignitaries of the church but also the two greatest Spanish authors of the time: Miguel de Cervantes and Lope de Vega. For she, who was here to be admitted into the ranks of the blessed, had been granted, together with the grace of divine visions, also the grace of the word. She had lived the life of a saint and with the genius of a great poet had known how to put her experience into words. The ineffable had befallen her. God had appeared to her in His substanceless essence. And the poet in her had found the words which carried it over into the realm of tangible forms. She found similes for that which nothing resembles, images for what no one imagined and words for what was told her without speech. Her comparisons and her metaphors were considered by Cervantes as "jewels of poetry." She was carried away by ecstasies. In her raptures she was raised into heaven. And the rhythm of her ecstasies and the bliss of her raptures were transposed by her into the rhythm and the beauty of her verses and stanzas.

Teresa de Cepeda, who was now a member of the community of the blessed, was a poet by the grace of God. Her fame as a poet is recognized in the history of letters and lives on through modern times, while her work as a saintly reformer of the order of the Carmelites is merely a factor in the history of the church. And yet, everything she wrote, with all its immortal beauties, was meant exclusively to be of service to her reform; it has been loved and admired by readers everywhere for close to four hundred years, but it was conceived in all humility for the benefit of a few discalced nuns.

Everything in Theresa's life is interdependent. The visionary cannot be separated from the patient, nor the practical reformer from the contemplative mystic. As the one was always caused and determined by the other, so also did the poet come to the fore through the militant nun.

When her plans for the foundation of her first convent became known and started a furious attack of abuse against her, her father confessor made her write down a complete confession which was to supply reliable and detailed information about the outer and inner course of her life. This was the occasion of the first version of her famous *Vida*. The second version, which is the one known today and which differs from the first in that it contains the story of Theresa's discalced foundations, was written at the official request of the Grand Inquisitor Francisco Soto y Salazar and was to assist the experts of the Holy Office in their investigation of the disputed case of the dissenting nun of the Carmelite order. This work Theresa composed while she was prioress of St. Joseph's at Ávila, after her day's work, when her nuns had gone to rest. At the time she was almost fifty and still ailing. In her little cell she had no chair, no table, no window panes. It was winter, and the biting Castilian wind blew through the canvas-covered frames. The old *madre* sat crouching on the tile floor, pressing the parchment against the window board and writing in great haste one sheet after another, often hardly able to move her painfully frost-bitten fingers. But she would not give in and sat there and wrote, night after night, often till dawn, often till it was time for her to get up and attend morning mass.

During these icy nights a masterpiece was composed on the window board of the little cell. She did not find the time to polish and cut, to remove grammatical errors and pay attention to correct punctuation. The whole manuscript of the *Vida*, as it is now kept at the Escorial, shows but fourteen corrections, but such flaws are more than made up for by literary merits, which no other autobiographical work of world literature can claim with the possible exception of St. Augustine's *Confessions*.

The keenness and penetration of her self-analysis amazes modern psychologists and induced the great Danish philosopher Harald Hoeffer to list St. Theresa among the founders of present-day psychology. The conciseness of her account of her illness is not surpassed by any modern pathography, and, aside from Dostoevski, no creative genius has equaled this saintly self-analyst of the sixteenth century in her masterly insight into the functional interdependence of disease and creative powers. Yet all these qualities of her work result simply from the endeavor of a God-fearing nun to present to her confessor and to her judges a factual confession in which nothing is withheld and nothing glossed over. Who reveals himself honestly, reveals himself fully. And thus there emerges from Theresa's *Vida* a complete and lifelike picture of her character—an extraordinary personality, a woman teeming with life, of great determination, humor and sensitivity. And precisely these traits of her character emerge also from her hundreds of fascinating letters, which have been collected in three heavy volumes.

Her confession was written for her confessor and for the Inquisition; for no one else. Her second work was conceived for her nuns. Immediately after the completion of her *Vida*, she began work on her *Way of Perfection*. Here she shows the way which she herself had found after many errors and much suffering. She, who had learned through experience, teaches the inexperienced step by step about the road which leads from vocal prayer to the prayer of silence, from meditation to contemplation, from physical asceticism to the highest form of spiritual asceticism, to the uttermost limits of human existence where the second realm begins in which the Lord Himself welcomes the pilgrim. For although Theresa had been exalted to the noble rank of sainthood by the grace of God, her conception of grace, like that of her contemporary St. Ignatius of Loyola, was deeply democratic, and she held that perfection is attainable for anyone who truly strives after it. She admonished her nuns to seek nothing but the highest: "God deliver you, sisters, from saying when you have done something that is not perfect: 'We are no angels, we are no saints.' Though we are not, it is the greatest help to believe that with God's aid we can be. This sort of presumption I wish to see in this house." And elsewhere: "It is true that His Majesty grants His favors to whom He chooses; yet if we sought Him as He seeks us, He would give them to all of us. He only longs for souls on whom He may bestow them, for His gifts do not diminish His riches."

Theresa who had herself been transformed and transfigured by exercises of prayer, imparted in the *Way of Perfection* her knowledge to her nuns. Her directions culminate in her discussion of the Lord's Prayer in which she succeeds in making her readers partake of the whole invigorating power of this prayer. Only Leo Tolstoi, the saint of Jasnaja Poljana, equals Theresa in her grasp of its spiritual immediacy.

The striking imagery, the originality of similes, the passionate eloquence, which are the literary qualities of this work, resulted from the practical endeavor of a prioress to show her nuns the way of perfection. Her mystical experience of God, however, could not be transmitted by the most convincing explanation, by the most exact prosaic description, and since she still wanted to share it with her daughters, she found for it, for their benefit, the poetic form of her hymns. Thus were conceived her most beautiful songs, the "Calls of the Soul to God," and her exquisite "Spiritual Canticles."

In 1577, ten years after the completion of the *Way of Perfection* and five years before her death, Theresa wrote at Toledo her third and last major work, *The Interior Castle*. Thus the story of her soul is rounded off as a trilogy; the mystic directions of the leader of the discalced Carmelite nuns are completed; and the unique art of constructive analysis of the poet Theresa attains consummate and classical perfection. This work, like her earlier ones, was written at the behest and for the benefit of the movement of her reform. Her confessor, Father Jerome Gracian, who meanwhile had been made general of the order of the discalced Carmelites, ordered her to reduce the mystic experiences of her reunion with God to a systematic presentation, suitable for the instruction of her nuns.

By order of one of her earlier confessors at Ávila, Theresa had told in her *Vida* the truthful and detailed story of God's grace and her visions; in her *Way of Perfection* she had showed her nuns the way of prayer which she herself had taken to God. And now Father Gracian requested from her a systematic account of her inner kingdom of God. She was keenly aware of the painful discrepancy between the experience of ecstasy and the verbal rendering of it. "Some of it," she writes, "is so sublime that it is not fitting for man, while living in this world, to understand it in a way that can be told; how this which we call *unio mystica* is effected and what it is I cannot tell. Mystical theology explains it, and I do not know the terms of science; nor can I understand what the mind is, nor how it differs from the soul or the spirit either."

When Father Gracian asked her to write *The Interior Castle*, she replied: "Why do you want me to write? Let learned men write who have studied, for I am a fool and won't know what I am saying: I will use one word in place of another, and I will do harm. There are plenty of books on these matters. For the love of God, I wish you would let me spin my flax, follow my chores and duties of religion, like the other sisters, for I am not fit for writing." And when she gave in and began her work in a spirit of obedience, she wrote the opening sentence: "I know not what to say nor how to commence this work which obedience has laid upon me."

Quite apart from the difficulty of the subject, the circumstances under which she commenced this work were the most unfavorable that could be imagined. The year 1577 was among the hardest of her life. It was a year of desperate struggles which she was forced to wage with tied hands. Her adversaries Tostado and Sega struck blow upon blow against the reform; the mitigation circulated calumniatory pamphlets against her; she was exiled to her convent at Toledo and condemned to restrict her fight for the reform to letter-writing. On the 2nd of June she began to write *The Interior Castle*. Two weeks later she had to interrupt and could resume her work only by the middle of November.

All these vicissitudes were aggravated by illness. An epidemic of influenza which had spread all over Spain broke Theresa's power of resistance, and when she finally recovered, her old ills came back with increased violence.

"I must tell you what is going on in my head," she says in *The Interior Castle*. "I suffer from noises which make it almost impossible for me to write about essential business. It seems as though many swollen rivers were rushing within my brain over a precipice; and then again, drowned by the noise of the water, are voices of birds singing and whistling. I weary my brain and increase my headaches by striving to obey."

Yet no sooner had she begun to write than she achieved the impossible and managed to describe the divine events which she had witnessed in her visions. The fitting expression for the inexpressible came with easy precision. The distinction between the various types of vision was carried through by this humble and untutored nun with a degree of lucidity which scholars later on have compared to that of the great scholastic thinker St. Thomas Aquinas. All external troubles vanished, the whole world of external events faded away while she was writing *The Interior Castle*. And even the interruption of full five months, which the struggle for the reform imposed upon her, seemed to last but one second. When she took up her work again, it was as though she were merely proceeding on a new sheet. The whole turmoil of rushing rivers, the singing and whistling of birds in her head, was silenced as soon as she set out to write about divine truth and the meaning of all creation. Let all physical ills torture her, the nun who was describing the treasure of her soul, did not feel her body. But then, was this really an ailing, untutored nun, who sat there writing? Ecstasy was writing for her! Ecstasy, which knows all words and similes and which has the power to express the inexpressible; which knows more about the distinctions between various kinds of vision than the most learned doctors of the church. And such ecstasy is not a thing of this world. Persecutions cannot harm it. Rushing waters and the twitter of birds cannot disturb it. Such ecstasy it was that wrote down on paper Theresa's *Interior Castle* in four short weeks.

Legend has it that a nun once entered Theresa's cell to deliver a message and found the madre sitting in front of a blank sheet of parchment. Theresa had not noticed that someone had entered and the nun observed she was in a trance. When Theresa came to again, the sheet was all covered with her forceful handwriting. In one of her letters to brother Lorenzo, Theresa described this ecstatic period in her life in her characteristically impressive style: "I go about these days like a drunkard in some ways."

On November 29th, 1577, the work was finished. "Although, as I told you," she says in the epilogue, "I felt reluctant to begin this work, yet now it is finished, I am very glad to have written it, and I think my trouble has been worthwhile, though I confess it has cost me but little. If anything in this book is to the point, you must understand that it did not originate in me and that there is no reason to attribute it to me; for with my scant understanding and skill I could write nothing of this sort, unless God, in His mercy, enabled me to do so."

The madre, whose only concern in life was to show her nuns the way to God, wrote this book, too, as she says, "only to my sisters; the idea that anyone else could benefit from it, would be absurd." But no sooner had Luis de Leon, one of the greatest poets of the Spanish renaissance, published her work by order of the king, than fame took it immediately upon its wings. And fame corrected her humbly erroneous verdict and incorporated the work, which was written for her nuns, in the treasure of the inalienable possessions of mankind.

Immortalized by posterity, the *madre* of a Spanish convent became the seraphic mother which we see in her today. Her spiritual descendants grew more numerous as the centuries rolled on. To the ranks of her discalced daughters were added popes and theologians, great poets and thinkers. Pascal and Malebranche, Leibnitz and even Voltaire, the apostle of skepticism, were among them. The truth of her teachings has not been shaken by centuries of scientific thought. She is the seraphic mother, today as yesterday and tomorrow, for all those who wish to transcend the ephemerality of ego and world, to start on the road of perfection to God. That the goal, toward which her road takes us, does actually exist, has been confirmed before and after her time by all the loftiest teachers of mankind: the Brahmins of the Upanishads eight hundred years before Christ; Sakyamani, the mystical teacher of Buddhism; St. Paul; the Neoplatonists; the mystics of the Middle Ages; the poets of Persian Sufism; and painters and poets as el Greco, Milton, Tennyson, William Blake, Francis Thompson.

But what made of the *madre* of Ávila the seraphic mother of the great chorus mysticus, is mainly her motherliness. In her writings a mother guides with loving hands the novice to the ultimate secrets of God. For Theresa not only knew the way but pursued it as a loving and motherly guide encouraging others to follow.

# Bibliography

## Saint Theresa

Barres, Maurice. *les Maitres*. Paris, 1927.

Bertrand, Louis. *Sainte Therese*. Paris, 1927.

Breysig, Kurt. *Die Geschichte der Seete*. Breslau, 1931.

Buber, Martin. *Ekstatische Konfessionen*. Jena, 1909.

Chesterton, Ada Elizabeth. *St. Teresa*. New York, 1928.

Crashaw, Richard. *Three Poems on St. Teresa*. London, 1938.

Forbes, Francis Alice. *The Life of Saint Teresa*. London, 1917.

Frost, Bede. *Saint John of the Cross*. London, 1937.

Graham, Gabriela Cunninghame. *Santa Teresa*. London, 1894.

Heiler, Friedrich. *Die Mystik im Leben der Kirche*. Munich, 1919.

Heiler, Friedrich. *Das Gebet, eine religionsgeschichtliche und religionspsychologische Untersuchung*. Munich, 1921.

Hocking, William Ernest. *The Meaning of God in Human Experience*. New Haven, 1912.

Hogan, John Gerard. *Heralds of the King*. Boston, 1934.

Hiigel, Friedrich Freiherr von. *The Mystical Element of Religion*. New York, 1909.

Jung, Carl Gustay. *Das Unbewusste im normalen and kranken Seelenleben*. Zurich, 1936.

Karrer, Otto. *Der mystische Strom*. Munich, 1926.

Leuba, James Henry. *The Psychology of Religious Mysticism*. New York, 1925.

MarZchal, Joseph. *Etudes sur la psychologie des mystiques*. 2 vls. Brussels, 1938.

Mariejol, Jean Hippolyte. *Philipp II*. New York, 1933.

Moore, Virginia. *Distinguished Women Writers*. New York, 1934.

Peers, Edgar Allison. *Studies of the Spanish Mystics*. 2 vls. London, 1927-3o.

Peers, Edgar Allison. *Spirit of Flame, a Study of St. John of the Cross*. London, 1944.

Riley, Isaac Woodbridge. *The Meaning of Mysticism*. New York, 1930.

Sackville-West, Victoria Mary. *The Eagle and the Dove*. New York, 1944.

Santayana, George. *The Genteel Tradition at Bay*. New York, 1931.

Sencourt, Robert Esmonde. *Carmelite and Poet, . . . Saint John of the Cross*. London, 1943.

Taylor, Henry Osborn. *Thought and Expression in the Sixteenth Century*. 2 vls. New York, I930.

Teresa, Saint. *La Vida*. Madrid, 1752.

Teresa, Saint. The Way of Perfection. London, 1911.

Teresa, Saint. *The Interior Castle*. London, 1912.

Underhill, Evelyn. *The Essentials of Mysticism*. London, 1920.

Underhill, Evelyn. *The Mystics of the Church*. London, 1925.

Walsh, William Thomas. *Philipp II*. London, 1937.

Walsh, William Thomas. *Saint Teresa of Avila*. Milwaukee, 1944.

# Other Books Written or Edited by Castellano-Hoyt

*dcastellano.hoyt@gmail.com*

*Bud Robinson Stories and Sketches*, Rev. C.T. Corbett

*Descriptive Outline of YOGODA*, Yogananda, Nerode

*How You Can Talk With God*, Yogananda

*It Can Be Done*, Ranendra Kumar Das

*Reincarnation*, Ranendra Kumar Das

*My Hospital Experience*, Rev. Bud Robinson

*Phineas F. Bresee: A Prince in Israel*
Rev. E.A. Girvin

*Scientific Healing Affirmations* Yogananda

*Stories of Mukunda*, Kriyananda

*The Eternal Religion*, Don Castellano-Hoyt

*Enhancing Police Response to Persons in Mental Health Crisis*
Don Castellano-Hoyt

*The Heathen Invasion*, Mabel Potter Daggett

*The Master Said*, Yogananda

*Yogiraj Shri Shri Lahiri Mahasaya*
Jogesh Bhattacharya

*Yogoda or Tissue-Will System System of Physical Perfection*
Yogananda

CPSIA information can be obtained
at www.ICGtesting.com
Printed in the USA
BVHW041802060719
552764BV00018B/843/P